THE BIG GAME

Benjamin Péret

Translated with an introduction
by Marilyn Kallet

Le gran jeu by Benjamin Péret © Éditions GALLIMARD, Paris, 1928, 2011. Published by arrangement with Éditions GALLIMARD. BWP wishes to thank Florence Giry for her help with this title.

Black Widow Press is an imprint of Commonwealth Books, Inc., Boston, MA. Distributed to the trade by NBN (National Book Network) throughout North America, Canada, and the U.K. All Black Widow Press books are printed on acid-free paper, and glued into bindings. Black Widow Press and its logo are registered trademarks of Commonwealth Books, Inc.

Joseph S. Phillips and Susan J. Wood, Ph.D, Publishers
www.blackwidowpress.com

Cover photo: Benjamin Péret, 1923, by Man Ray © Man Ray Trust /ADAGP - ARS / Telimage - 2011.
Typesetting: Kerrie Kemperman

ISBN-13: 978-0981808864

Printed in the United States

10 9 8 7 6 5 4 3 2 1

For Joe Phillips and Susan Wood

CONTENU

LE GRAND JEU

CONTENTS

LE QUART D'UNE VIE

LA PÊCHE EN EAU TROUBLE

LE TRAVAIL ANORMAL

QUARTER OF A LIFE

FISHING IN TROUBLED WATER

ABNORMAL WORK

LE PASSAGER DU TRANSATLANTIQUE

THE TRANSATLANTIC PASSENGER

A André Breton

To André Breton

ACKNOWLEDGEMENTS

Joe Phillips at Black Widow Press has done American letters a great service by opening our pages to Dadaist and Surrealist literature in translation. He has been particularly supportive of my poetry and translations over the years. I am honored to be part of his amazing list of authors and translators.

Production of *The Big Game* was made possible in part by grants from the John C. Hodges Better English Fund, the College of Arts & Sciences, and the University of Tennessee Office of Research through the Exhibit, Publication and Performance Expenses Fund. Over the years, the Hodges Fund and the Professional Development Fund of the Graduate School have supported my writing and research in France. Professors Charles Maland, Stan Garner, Michael Keene, John Zomchick, and Carolyn Hodges, Vice Provost and Dean of the University of Tennessee Graduate School, have encouraged my translating of modern and contemporary French poetry.

The Virginia Center for the Creative Arts has provided writing residencies for me in Auvillar, France, and in Sweet Briar, Virginia, where I have worked on this project. I also worked on translations at Cassilhaus, in Chapel Hill. I will always be grateful.

My research assistant, Darren Jackson, a fine poet and translator in his own right, helped with editing and formatting the manuscript. Parisian poet Chantal Bizzini offered insights and editorial suggestions. Other friends kindly assisted with the revisions: Laurence Baudry and Pauline Beauruel were particularly helpful. Abdoulaye Yansané made suggestions on an early version of the manuscript. To these poets and translators I am indebted. I have also enjoyed discussing Péret's idiosyncratic vocabulary with French speakers on the forums at WordReference.com.

For my translations I have used the Gallimard edition of *Le grand jeu,* 1928, updated in 1969, with a preface by Robert Benayoun. I am grateful for their permission to reprint the French poems. The dedication page, to André Breton, is found in the first volume of the complete works, published by the Association des amis de Benjamin Péret, under the Eric Losfeld imprint.

The most helpful source on Benjamin Péret was Mark Polizzotti's *Revolution of the Mind: The Life of André Breton,* 1995, updated and republished by Black Widow Press, 2009. This volume is like rich chocolate cake, and slices on the life of Breton also include news of Péret, who was Breton's most loyal friend. I admire the introductory essay to Benjamin Péret by Péret's younger friend, Jean-Louis Bedoin, published by Seghers in 1957. This generous personal essay offers enlightening details about Péret's background and tastes. There is little background material available on Péret, and some of what exists is either overly poetic—Benayoun's preface to the Gallimard edition of *Le grand jeu,* for example, in which Péret can do no wrong—or prosaic, as in the case of translator Elizabeth Jackson's introduction to her sampler of Péret poems, *A Marvelous World* (L.S.U. Press, 1985).

My chronology builds upon facts listed by the dedicated scholars at Association des amis de Benjamin Péret: http://www.benjamin-peret.org/. I am grateful to this organization for encouraging interest in the work of Péret.

INTRODUCTION

In the opening round of Benjamin Péret's *The Big Game,* the narrator grows winded over good cheese and a good woman who seems to blend with the dairy products. Péret's "Breathlessly" ("S'essoufler") spins a preschool song into a kind of pantoum. The traditional ditty offers cheerful repetition and bounce, not unlike "The Farmer in the Dell." This children's song summons village housewives, "Ah, Mesdames, voilà du bon fromage!" "Ah, Ladies, here's some great cheese!" Péret reverses the order of things, sighs to the cheese that there's a fine lady on the scene. We expect no less from a Surrealist, as the Surrealists were former Dadaist-Tricksters and remained love poets par excellence. Péret was known for dark humor, but "S'essoufler" stays "cheesy" and sunny. The poet whips up the pace by omitting punctuation; his verses whirl by like a folk song on speed.

This first poem brags about being homemade, provincial, like its maker, Benjamin Péret, who was born in Western France, in Rezé, and grew up in Nantes. Péret was the quintessential Surrealist, one who never compromised his love for freedom of imagination, not for any cause or material gain. He spent much of his adult life in poverty. If images of food surged from Péret's pen, these probably reflected actual hunger. Uncompromising in friendship, too, Péret was one of the few original members of the Dadaist and then Surrealist group who stayed loyal to the founder, André Breton. The two remained lifelong friends—a hard trick with Breton, who continually bumped writers and artists, including Eluard and Picasso, from his circle and his life. Péret dedicated *Le grand jeu* to André Breton.[1]

The poet was shy, an outsider in Paris. According to his friend Robert Desnos, Péret's mother brought her son to Breton's apartment at Place du Pantheon, early one January morning in 1920. Her boy, she said, needed

19

career advice. Breton's more romantic version of this meeting is included in *Nadja,* where "late one night" a mysterious woman in black knocked on his door; her mission was to acquire a copy of *Littérature* to take back to Nantes. Péret himself turned up a few days later.[2] Either way, Péret quickly became involved in the Dadaist manifestations, helped to man the research office at Surrealist Central (though Eluard complained that Péret often didn't show up), and with Pierre Naville became one of the first editors of the magazine, *La Révolution Surréaliste.*

If Péret's milk-and-cheese opening act in *The Big Game* sounds family-friendly, his poetry was not always rated squeaky clean. In 1929, with Aragon and Man Ray, Péret contributed poetry to a fundraising project for the Surrealist magazine, *Variétés.* The project, *1929,* was a book of graphic photos of sexual intercourse with accompanying verse.[3] The volume was banned in France, and confiscated at its borders. More often than explicit sexual imagery in *The Big Game,* though, the reader will find vocabulary of weather and flora. But the weather is sudden and capricious, and will keep the reader alert.

Breath. Wind. Sudden transformations of landscape and of the ordinary world. In this collection's second poem, "Watch Out for the Desert Wind" ("Attention au simoun"), dedicated to Picasso, there's heat and movement. Everything is dynamic in Péret's poetry. The Muse is not one person or thing, but a force, like the Jerry Lee Lewis song, "Great Balls of Fire," now an epic wind and a Saharan vista with a dog day sun, now a street musician with three accordions that have minds of their own. There's generative magic in Péret's lyrics. Images seem to breed, and sometimes, in sudden shifts the postmodernists would appreciate, images turn to mechanical engineering terms, or to smoke. A Péret poem is a line-by-line reclamation of experience through imagination, which "recovers" skeletons in their skins.

Péret reanimates poetry with slang phrases and skewed idioms, forcing staleness from worn speech. The poet finds lyrical freedom when "liberté" beds "égalité"—when the poetry of vernacular speech becomes an intimate part of a genre that might have been deemed elitist prior to the Surrealists.

"Vilaine va" ("Bad girl, scram"), he spits, punctuating lines on French political ideals with idiomatic language one might use toward a dog ("Portrait de Robert Desnos"). And in "Downfall of the Bodies" ("La chute des corps"), Péret changes the saying "J'ai un poil dans la main" ("I am lazy") to "J'ai un poil dans la tête," which creates nonsense. The image devolves into the next line, where the saying, "J'ai rien dans la carafe" ("I'm empty-headed") becomes "Il n'y en a pas autant dans la carafe" ("There's not as much in the carafe"). "I'm a few more beers short of a six pack," we might say, and the self-mocking line continues the playful trend of bending idioms throughout the poem. Péret's lines evoke the liberating anarchy of the Fugs' song, "Monday nothing/Tuesday nothing…Thursday and Friday a little more nothing…"[4]

Lively, often funny, Péret's fugue of images can turn serious. In "Cloud," for example, what kind of "gingerbread" looms, linked to sickness in the landscape and wounds to the population? It may help to know that the odor of some poison gas (chloropicrin) used in World War I has been compared to the smell of gingerbread. By contrast, many Péret poems create their own mood of genesis—"Samson" unfolds with an epic sweep to the lines and a prophetic tone; the poets' fingers become the "springs" for a torrent of images. Sullen glances are banned from this poem, for fear they might be "mirrored," contagious.

Like a jazz musician playing improvisations, Péret listened to his thoughts with clairvoyant expectation, leaned in and took dictation. As a participant in the hypnotic trances or "sleeping fits" at Breton's apartment in 1922, he experienced with Desnos and René Crevel the power of the unconscious to drive the poems. He practiced automatic writing; the poems from *Le passager du transatlantique* were among the earliest automatic writing done by Péret's hand.

The Big Game as a whole is up-tempo; language tries to keep up with the current of images coursing through the entranced or daydreaming brain. Charles Olsen might have approved of this "instanter." Like the other provincial, Rimbaud, who ran through his life and poems, Péret leaps in his lines from one image to the next, trying to get ahead of his rational mind, to keep surprising the unknown. Early on, Péret expressed admiration for Mallarmé,[5] whose compression and aesthetic control might seem contrary to the spirit of Surrealism. Yet the structure of Péret's poems is usually quite logical. Within coherent syntax, Péret shapes worlds of images that are fluid, in metamorphosis. By the 1920s, Péret had discovered Rimbaud, who was much admired by the Dadaists and then by the Surrealists. Rimbaud, along with Apollinaire, Jarry, and Lautréamont, overrode Mallarmé, leaving Péret to paint windows of vivid images without obvious frames.

The accomplishment of Péret's lyrics astonishes all the more when we remember that he did not even attend the lycée. In 1914, at fifteen, he was caught with his friends vandalizing a town statue, and was given a choice of signing up for the army or going to jail. His mother insisted on the army. At sixteen, Péret was deployed to the Balkans. On a railway bench he found a copy of the literary magazine, *Sic,* which contained poetry by Apollinaire. In Salonica he became seriously ill with dysentery, and was sent to Lorraine, where he remained until the end of the war.

Péret found his own childhood unremarkable, and was not interested in poetry as memoir.[6] Nevertheless, we can't help but notice anti-military and anti-clerical threads in his work. In Paris, Péret overcame his reserved temperament to harass priests on the streets and buses. He went out of his way to spit on priests and to curse them.[7] The reader wonders whether there was something more personal than anti-clerical ideology behind these episodes. In any event, Dadaism gave Péret a way of ritualizing his loathing, a way of making theatre out of disdain.

His scorn for nationalism and for the military manifested itself dramatically in Paris, on May 13, 1921, at Salle des Sociétés Savantes, when he appeared as the "Unknown Soldier" in the Dadaist's mock trial of conservative Maurice Barrès. Péret goose-stepped into the room, wearing a German uniform and a gas mask, shouting rudimentary phrases in German. The audience jeered, rose to sing the *Marseillaise,* and some men rushed the stage. Breton, the presiding judge, must have been delighted. Péret barely escaped unharmed. Though he became known for this episode, Benjamin Péret was much more than a provocateur and a clown. "Dada est mort!" he shouted three times in "A travers mes yeux" ("Through my eyes"). In *Littérature*, April 1922, he announced he was taking off Dada "eyeglasses" for wherever the "wind might go."[8]

Péret created an impressive body of work—poetry, stories, political essays, and critical writings on art and film. In his essay, *La parole est á Péret (Péret's Turn to Speak)*, the poet reflected on his months in prison in Rennes. He had been called up in 1939, and while in the army had continued to participate in leftist political activities. In May 1940, he was imprisoned, then freed on June 21 as the German army approached. During his incarceration, Péret passed the time by staring at his cell window; he would imagine stained glass that opened scenes from French history and art. A meditation on poetry's power to free the human spirit in tribal and contemporary life, Péret's essay served as the preface to his edited collection of South American tribal poetry, *L'Anthologie des mythes, legendes et contes populaires d'Amérique*. The essay includes a short slang dictionary that is in itself a poem.[9] The project was endorsed in May 1943, by international writers and artists, among them Leonora Carrington, Aimé Césaire, André Breton, Marcel Duchamp, Matta, Max Ernst, and Yves Tanguy. In his endorsement, Breton pointed to Péret as one whose life was "singularly free of concessions." Breton noted as well that Péret was ahead of his time in his interest in ethnopoetics. Among other projects related to the oral tradition, Péret translated the Mayan epic, *Le Chilám Balám of Chumayal*, from Spanish into French.

Péret's connections to Mexico and South America were personal as well as cultural. He was married twice, to women who were accomplished artists in their own right. In 1928, the year *The Big Game* was published, he married Brazilian soprano Elsie Houston. They lived together in Brazil, and their son Geyser was born in Rio in 1931. (Péret joked that he wanted to call the boy "Deserter," but his wife wouldn't let him.) That year they were expelled from Brazil for communist activities. They moved to Paris, where Elsie became a cabaret performer; Péret worked as a proofreader. In 1936, he went to Spain to fight in the Civil War, first with the Marxist P.O.U.M. and with the anarchist Durutti column. By this time the couple had unofficially separated. Elsie Houston established a career in New York, where she created a nightclub act involving popular music, blues, and macumba (called "voodoo" by the press.) She died in New York, in March 1943, an apparent suicide.

In 1946, Péret married painter Remedios Varo, whom he had met in Barcelona during the Spanish war. The two had escaped the Nazis in 1941 by fleeing France via Marseilles, bound for Mexico. They were stranded for months in Casablanca before finally getting the papers they needed to travel to Vera Cruz. In Mexico, Remedios Varo became close friends with Leonora Carrington, the Surrealist writer and painter. Varo's paintings show affinities with the work of Max Ernst and de Chirico; they feature magical buildings and alchemical machines. Their predominant color is gold. But Péret returned to Paris alone in 1948. No doubt it was difficult for the women to be married to the most unworldly Surrealist, difficult also to have been artists kept outside a circle that most often viewed women as lovers, wives, and muses—not as creative equals.

In Mexico, Péret had composed another important essay, *Le déshonneur des poètes*. There he spoke out against chaining poetry to any goal. He railed against his old friends Eluard and Aragon for writing political poetry during World War II, poetry that seemed to him no better than pharmaceutical advertising. In particular, he quoted Eluard's famous poem, "Liberté," which was leafleted over France by the R.A.F. during the war. Péret thought that the incantatory nature of this poem turned it into liturgy.

Péret's own poetry often uses repeated phrases—for example, "que n'avait-il" ("why didn't he") in "Spilled Blood" ("Le sang répandu")— but his lyrics question the action, deflate the surge of imagery. Péret wanted poetry to answer only to language and discovery, not to any cause, not even to the cause of freedom. He pronounced poetry's absolute importance, "If we delve into the original meaning of poetry...we note that it is the true breath (souffle) of man..." (*Le déshonneur des poètes*).[10] His essay reads like a love letter to poetry, and also, implicitly, to his friend André Breton, who had initiated the Surrealist movement.

Can we look into the fanciful poems of *The Big Game* and predict the survivor of wars and prisons, the theorist and translator of the Mayan epic? We have noted that images of breath and wind launch the book, and that vernacular language peppers the lines. Each poem lets imagination hold sway, a practice that became sustaining in times of hardship. Though theoretically Péret's allegiance evolved from Dadaism to Surrealism, in harmony with Breton and their circle of poets and painters, it is difficult to see any major shift within the poems themselves, which are enlivened by barrages of strange images. As Breton said, "Always for the first time I hardly know you by sight"—a line that might apply not just to the sight of a beloved woman, but to imagery that continues to startle, poem after poem.

Péret's political affiliations were complex and kept getting him in trouble—he moved back and forth from Marxism and the Worker's Party to becoming a Trotskyite, then back to the party. Many French intellectuals, among them Breton and Eluard, were idealistic about communism in the years before Stalin's purges. Eluard even wrote an ode to Stalin. For Péret, the political track ran parallel to the poetry, and did not burden the poems of *The Big Game,* which sail like paper lanterns, weightless.

If his poems are so agile, why isn't Benjamin Péret better known in Europe and in America? Schoolchildren in France read poems by Eluard, but not by Péret. Contemporary French poets know Péret's work, but French readers in general do not even recognize his name. This may be because of Péret's loyalty to Surrealism, to the dynamics of imagery rather than to narrative or song, and to the fact that he never wrote to be popularly read. Maybe his role as a Dadaist provocateur stamped him as untouchable by the bourgeoisie. Since the late 1940s, the Association des amis de Benjamin Péret has sought to redress the lack of recognition in France, and has published seven volumes of his collected works in poetry and prose.[11]

American readers have even less familiarity with Péret's writings than readers in France. For one thing, his work has not been translated in its entirety. Elizabeth Jackson and Keith Holloman have translated selections of poetry from different collections, including *Le grand jeu,* and happily these translations appear with the French alongside. Other works of prose published by Black Swan Press have been translated without the French accompanying, making it harder for readers to taste the flavor of the original. Black Widow Press is working to redress the lack of key texts by bringing into print Dadaist and Surrealist authors in translation, with the original French en face.

Surrealist art has become part of American life through our major museums and galleries, but the writings remain less known. America's Puritan background tends to make us suspicious of daydreaming. "No ideas but in things," William Carlos Williams asserted, though he too was a great dreamer, especially toward the end of his life. "The American Dream" is one of material and social success. By contrast, the Surrealists honored dreaming and free association over linear thinking, over the conscious mind. In America, advertising has appropriated the techniques of Surrealist art wholesale, using dream imagery to manage our associations. Péret's line "Changing of meat gladdens the pigs," showcased in "Charcutons Charcutez," might be appropriated today for Chik-fil-A billboards.

From New York, where he lived during the war, André Breton wrote to his old friend Benjamin Péret, complaining about the crassness of American culture: "No curiosity about anything that isn't immediately commercial; no respect for the written word…"[12] Péret was then living in Mexico with Remedios Varo and their son Geyser. In 1948, Breton took care of his impoverished friend by sending him the money to return to Paris. Péret later traveled back to Brazil, where he lived with tribal people in the Amazon rain forest and worked on his anthology of myths and legends during 1955–56. He was arrested there on an old warrant for political activities; thanks to an international effort by writers and by the press on his behalf, he was released to go home to France.

Having neglected his health for years, his condition became more and more precarious. He was hospitalized and operated on for blocked arteries in the spring of 1959. Benjamin Péret died of a heart failure in Boucicaut hospital in Paris, September 18, 1959, and was buried on September 24, in the Parisian cemetery of Batignolles.

As a translator, I came to Péret's work with a bias toward love songs. Having translated Paul Eluard's *Last Love Poems (Derniers poèmes d'amour)*, I had been won over by Eluard's musicality, by his lyrics that communicated joy and grief. I admired him for hiding in Paris with his wife Nusch during the war, respected him for writing and publishing for the Resistance.[13]

While Eluard relied on the intimate "you" in his lyrics, directing his lines to the beloved, Péret's work seemed less personal, less concerned with communicating. Péret did not use first person to confide personal feelings; it would be hard to imagine couples incorporating his poetry as wedding vows the way they turn to Eluard's love poems. Yet Péret was no less ambitious than Eluard in his poetic vision.

Péret's lines evoke alternative worlds, where poetry rivals nature: "Pour être égal des plantes/il faut être grand dans la vie/et solide dans le mort…" ("To be the equal of plants/one must be large in life/and solid in death." There's a "sun" in Péret's imagination that rivals the daybreak, "The sun of my head's in every color…" ("Les temps révolus") ("The Distant Past"). We translators and readers are offered myriad glimpses into a creative mind in the act of generating landscapes of fantastical images.

Quirky images spring up, poem after poem. Perhaps Péret named his son Geyser because he loved the verb "jaillir," to spurt. His antic lines make us laugh aloud. Though Breton edited an anthology of dark humor, *Anthologie de l'humour noir*,[14] his own work does not offer much laughter. Nor does Eluard's, unless he's in the company of Péret (*152 Proverbes mis au goût du jour*, 1925).[15] Péret's poetry doesn't idealize women the way Breton's did, or eroticize them as in Eluard's work. Unfortunately, Péret can be guilty of creating images that are dated and suspect with reference to people of color. "The winks of negroes" in "Smoked Ears Will Not Grow Back" is a troubling example of such imagery.

In many ways, though, Péret's work sounds contemporary. In "The Marriage of Leaves," he notes that the language of his "circular" poetry "pitches and rolls/like botanical waves." If he were alive today, he might enjoy taking nature walks in the California hills with Robert Hass. He could engage in anti-war activity with Brenda Hillman, and discuss French cave art with Clayton Eshleman. He would enjoy the Dadaist "Ghost Tantras" of Michael McClure, the prose poems of Russell Edson, and the anthologies of oral tradition poetry by Jerome Rothenberg. He would want a front row seat for Joy Harjo's performances. He and Yusef Komunyakaa might talk about daydreaming as a survival strategy in times of war. He would not need a translator for "Dream Machine," the exhibit of collages by Brion Gysin and William S. Burroughs at the New Museum of Contemporary Art in New York.[16]

Childhood stories prepared me for the thrilling instability of Péret's images. When I was three or four years old, my mother used to read aloud one Uncle Wiggly story each night before bed. Each story ended with a series of silly transformations, and with a promise of more: "And if the boiled egg doesn't try to go sailing in the gravy boat, and splash condensed milk on the bread-knife, I'll tell you on the page after this about Uncle Wiggly and the Stubby Toes."[17] Péret keeps the reader in suspense, too, as in "The Memoirs of Benjamin Péret,"

> Up top the ladder broke
> The ladder became a fat mailman
> The cow fell into criminal court
> The cats played *La Madelon*
> and the rest went into a newspaper for unwed mothers.

Uncle Wiggly with a difference! If there's an undercurrent of "jouissance" or orgasm in *Le grand jeu,* it grows stronger in this poem as the mailman looks suspiciously fat; "cats" play a popular song about a barmaid; the poem's surplus (which starts out as breasts) falls to plural pregnant women, who may in turn find themselves reading Péret.[18] The reader can best appreciate Péret for his exuberant, vigorous imagery, for his wit and sense of discovery in *The Big Game*. Whether it's Uncle Wiggly who holds the mother and the storybook near the child's bed, keeps the lights on a few moments longer—or a savvy Scheherazade—we readers and listeners love stories for the ways they entrance us, keep us from dwelling on the limits of our world. Benjamin Péret's odd and varied poems generate worlds of song and story, sustaining us and helping us dreamers to keep our eyes open.

—Marilyn Kallet
2011

[1] *Oeuvres complètes*, 1. Association des amis de Benjamin Péret, Eric Losfeld, 1969, 69.

[2] The Desnos version is cited in Polizzotti, *Revolution of the Mind: The Life of André Breton*, Black Widow Press, 2009, 135; Breton, *Nadja*, Editions Gallimard, 1928; 1963, 26–27.

[3] Man Ray, Benjamin Péret, Louis Aragon, *Editions de la Revue Variétés*, 1929.

[4] "Nothing," Tuli Kupferberg, on *The Village Fugs*, Broadside, 1965.

[5] "Benjamin Péret par Jean-Louis Bedoin," in *Benjamin Péret*, Seghers, 1957.

[6] Bédoin, 19–22.

7   David Gascoyne mentions an incident that he personally witnessed on a Paris bus. *Remove Your Hat & Other Works*, Atlas Press, 1936; 1986, ix–x.

8   Bédoin, 27.

9   The anthology was published posthumously in Paris, 1960, by Albin Michel. The essay with its list of slang terms appeared first in *Péret: Le déshonneur des poètes précédé de la parole est á Péret*, ed. J.J. Pauvert, Association des amis de Benjamin Péret et La Terrain Vague, 1945, note 1, 28–29.

10 *Le déshonneur des poètes*, 71.

11 Most of Péret's writings are included in the *Oeuvres complètes;* the first four volumes, poetry, stories, and collaborative works, were published by Eric Losfeld, between 1950–1982. Tomes 5–7, including political essays, correspondence, essays, film and art criticism, were published by Editions Jose Corti, between 1989 and 1995.

12 Quoted in Polizzotti, *Revolution of the Mind: The Life of André Breton*, 456.

13 *Last Love Poems of Paul Eluard*, trans. M. Kallet, Black Widow Press, 2006.

14 Gallimard, 1939.

15 *La Révolution Surréaliste*, 1925; Eric Losfeld, 1972.

16 "The Unknown Loved by the Knowns," *The New York Times*, Art, Sunday, June 27, 2010, 21.

17 *Uncle Wiggily's Story Book*, Howard R. Garis, Platt-Monk, 1921; 1939, 63.

18 Of "jouissance" Jacques Lacan wrote, "It starts with a tickle and ends up bursting into flames." *The Ethics of Psychoanalysis*, 1991, 83.

LE GRAND JEU

THE BIG GAME

S'ESSOUFFLER

A Max Morise.

Ah fromage voilà la bonne madame
Voilà la bonne madame au lait
Elle est du bon lait du pays qui l'a fait
Le pays qui l'a fait était de son village

Ah village voilà la bonne madame
Voilà la bonne madame fromage
Elle est du pays du bon lait qui l'a fait
Celui qui l'a fait était de sa madame

Ah fromage voilà du bon pays
Voilà du bon pays au lait
Il est du bon lait qui l'a fait du fromage
Le lait qui l'a fait était de sa madame

BREATHLESSLY

To Max Morise

Ah cheese here's the good lady
Here comes the good lady with milk
She's from fresh milk from the land that made it
The land that made it came from her village

Ah village here's the good lady
Here comes good madam cheese
She's from the land of fresh milk that made it
The one who made it came from her lady

Ah cheese here's some good country
Here's some good milky country
It's from fresh milk that made it of cheese
The milk that made it came from her lady.

ATTENTION AU SIMOUN

A Picasso.

La chaleur pousse du brasier de saules
arrache les herbes et les plumes de la cervelle du pirate

Le pirate est un homme de taille
qui envie les arbres à cause de leurs oiseaux
et roule sur les dunes comme une pierre à fusil
Il attend sur le rocher sévère
debout au milieu des merveilles
que la main s'éloigne comme la terre du navire qui la fuit
Il attend que les yeux de ses maîtresses
renaissent des glands qui les simulent
Il attend que les flocons de neige tombés à ses pieds
s'envolent comme des mouches
Il attend que la chair recouvre les squelettes
et les squelettes recouvrent la campagne
recouvrent la chair des héros au nez fendu par le rire
recouvrent les villes tourmentées par les ornements
sacerdotaux
courent après les nuages qui se tordent comme des serpents
et fixent les miroirs obsédants

Pirate tu es un squelette et le plus pâle le plus fragile le plus lumineux
celui dont les bergers disent les pieds dans l'eau
Voici un beau mariage Comme il semble l'aimer
Pirate tu es un squelette
un de ceux qu'on devine chaque jour
sous les apparences de la raison
un de ceux qui s'ennuient devant une fontaine
et demandent une danseuse jolie à rougir
nue sous un manteau de sel

WATCH OUT FOR THE DESERT WIND

To Picasso

Heat grows from the inferno of willows
Rips weeds and feathers from the pirate's brain

The pirate's a man of measure
who envies trees their birds
and rolls on the dunes like a flintstone
He waits on the severe crag
standing amidst marvels
that his hand distances like land from the ship that flees it
He waits for his mistresses' eyes
to revive again like acorns that imitate them
He waits for snowflakes fallen at his feet
to take off like flies
He waits for flesh to cover up the skeletons
and for skeletons to cover the countryside
cover the flesh of heroes their nose split with laughter
cover the cities tormented by priestly ornaments
run after clouds that twist themselves like serpents
and stare at haunting mirrors.

Pirate you are a skeleton and the palest most fragile most luminous
the one of whom shepherds speak their feet in the water
Here's a fine marriage How he seems to love her
Pirate you are a skeleton
one of those that we guess each day
in the guise of reason
one of those who grow bored before a fountain
and ask for a dancer blushingly pretty
naked beneath a cloak of salt

LE MALADE IMAGINAIRE

Je suis le cheveu de plomb
qui tombe d'astre en astre
et deviendra la comète
qui te détruira dans un an et un jour

Maintenant il n'y a ni jour ni année
il y a une plante impeccable
dont tu voudrais être l'égal

pour être l'égal des plantes
il faut être grand dans la vie
et solide dans la mort
Or je suis seul immobile et muet comme un astre
les pieds baignant dans les nuages
qui comme autant des bouches
me condamnent à rester parmi les êtres immobiles
désespoir des plantes

Pourtant un jour les liquides révoltés
jailliront vers les nuages
armes meurtrières
maniées par des femmes bleus
comme les yeux des filles du nord

Et ce jour-là sera dans un an et un jour

THE HYPOCHONDRIAC

I am the strand of lead
that falls star to star
and will become the comet
that will smash you in a year and a day

Now there's neither day nor year
there's an impeccable plant
of which you'd love to be the equal

To be the equal of plants
one must be large in life
and solid in death
But I am lonely immobile and mute like a star
my feet bathing in clouds
which like so many mouths
condemn me to stay among inert beings
despair of plants

However one day rebellious liquids
will spurt toward the clouds
murderous weapons
maddened by blue women
like the eyes of northern girls

And that day will be in a year and a day

LES TEMPS RÉVOLUS

Le soleil de ma tête est de toutes les couleurs
C'est lui qui brûle les maisons
de paille
où vivent les seigneurs échappés des cratères
et les belles dames qui naissent chaque matin
et meurent chaque soir
comme les moustiques
Moustique de toutes les couleurs
que viens-tu faire ici
Il fait un soleil de chien
et la houle secoue les montagnes
maintenant que les montagnes
nagent sur une mer de lumière
une mer sans vie sans poids sans chaleur
où je ne mettrai pas le bout de mon pied

THE DISTANT PAST

The sun of my head's in all colors
That's who burns the houses
of straw
where noblemen live escaped from craters
and pretty women who are born each morning
and die each night
like mosquitoes
Mosquito in all colors
what did you come here for
It's fierce sun a dog day
and the swell shakes the mountains
now that the mountains
swim on a sea of light
a sea without life without weight without warmth
where I won't put the tip of my toe

A TRAVERS LE TEMPS ET L'ESPACE

Attendre sous le vent et la neige des astres
la venue d'une fleur indécente sur mon front décoloré
comme un paysage déserté par les oiseaux appelés soupirs du sage
et qui volent dans le sens de l'amour
voilà mon sort
voilà ma vie
Vie que la nature a faite pleine de plumes
et de poisons d'enfants
je suis ton humble serviteur

Je suis ton humble serviteur et je mords les herbes des nuages
que tu me tends sur un coussin
qui
comme une cuisse immortelle
conserve sa chaleur première et provoque le désir
que n'apaiseront jamais
ni la flamme issue d'un monstre inconsistant
ni le sang de la déesse
voluptueuse malgré la stérilité d'oiseau des marécages intérieurs

ACROSS TIME AND SPACE

Awaiting beneath the wind and snow of stars
the arrival of an obscene flower on my faded brow
like a landscape deserted by the birds called sighs of the sage
and which fly in the direction of love
there's my fate
there's my life
Life that nature has made full of feathers
and of poisons of children
I am your humble servant

I am your humble servant and I bite the weeds of clouds
that you offer me on a cushion
which
like an immortal thigh
keeps its first warmth and provokes desire
that will never ease
either the flame coming from an inconsistent monster
or the blood of the goddess
voluptuous despite the sterility of the bird of interior bayous

LES OREILLES FUMÉES NE REPOUSSERONT PLUS

Jadis une banane habituée au chenil
sautait les haies de son cerveau
cataracte de poissons perdus dans la montagne
Jadis les plumes des nuages s'envolaient
si loin que nul navigateur
malgré la pluie de suie et les œillades des nègres
ne les pouvait saisir comme un coquillage amoureux
Jadis les eaux salées dansaient
et les forets des pauvres roulaient sur les versants
mais aujourd'hui que les fontaines blanches
ont jeté dans les vallons les doigts de leurs ancêtres
que les routes ont tué leurs 70 animaux
que les saisons s'ennuient comme des prisonnières
que les souffles usés des plantes de la mer
ont rejeté dans les cavernes de la folie
les enfants blonds du réséda
une femme les cheveux teintés par ses songes
se promène dans les déserts et regarde les puits
O puits de mes amies vous êtes des oiseaux
et les oiseaux de mon cœur vous entourent
Ils sont bleus verts rouges incolores et sans saveur
ils ont la forme de mes ongles
et sont aussi nombreux que mes chiffres
O puits de mes amies vous êtes des syllabes
qui courent le long des falaises
des liquides perdus dans un nuage sonore
et je vous attends au bord de la figure VII
où les anneaux de mes yeux s'enchaînent comme des fleurs
où le bruit de mes pas croît comme une catapulte

SMOKED EARS WILL NOT GROW BACK

Once a banana accustomed to the kennel
jumped the hedges of its brain
cataract of fish lost in the mountain
Once the feathers of clouds flew off
so far that no navigator
despite the rain of soot and winks of negroes
could seize them like an amorous shellfish
Once the salty waters danced
and forests of the poor rolled on the slopes
but now that the white fountains
have thrown into valleys the fingers of their ancestors
that the roads have killed their 70 animals
that the seasons are bored like prisoners
that the worn sighs of the sea plants
have thrown back into caverns of madness
the blonde children of the mignonette
a woman with hair dyed by her dreams
strolls in the desert and looks at the wells
Oh wells of my girlfriends you are birds
and the birds of my heart surround you
They are blue green red colorless and without flavor
They take the shape of my fingernails
and are as numerous as my ciphers
Oh wells of my girlfriends you are syllables
which run along the cliffs
of liquids lost in a sonorous cloud
and I wait for you at the edge of the figure VII
where the rings of my eyes link like flowers
where the noise of my steps grows like a catapult

L'AVENIR EST AUX AUDACIEUX

Sous les pas de l'horizon
se creuse le puits d'amour
qu'on appelle vesce de moine

O puits qui rends visibles les étoiles à midi
et le soleil dans les cheveux des saisons
j'attends le jour simple comme un fruit
où légère une certaine Arcadie
descendant le long de l'horizon
offrira aux enfants de l'éclipse mortelle
son corps vierge et nu
marqué entre les seins d'un signe égalitaire

THE FUTURE BELONGS TO THE BOLD

Below the steps of the horizon
digs itself the well of love
called monk's weed

Oh well that makes stars visible at noon
and sun in the hair of seasons
I wait for the day simple like a fruit
where lightly a certain Arcadia
descending the horizon's length
will offer the children of mortal eclipse
her virgin and nude body
stamped between its breasts with an egalitarian sign

LES BEAUTÉS DU CIEL ET DE LA TERRE

Un grand monsieur aux cheveux salés
voulait être musicien
mais il était seul dans la vallée
avec trois accordéons

Le premier accordéon achevait de pourrir
Dans la simplicité de son âme
il aurait voulu être cheval
mais il y avait une lampe qui brûlait
qui brûlait

Le second accordéon tremblait
comme une maison au passage de sa sœur
C'est qu'il était une grande ville
qui trompait ses habitants
avec son maire
bête comme un pied de biche

Le troisième accordéon
aurait dévoré la terre et les oiseaux
s'il en avait eu l'envie
Mais c'était un sage
à la manière des orties
et il se contentait d'envier les animaux immobiles

Mais me direz-vous
le monsieur qui voulait être musicien

Il avait eu le temps de mourir
et le loisir de fumer
et c'était cette fumée qui montait de la terre vers les nuages

UNE TROMBE PAR TRIBORD

THE BEAUTIES OF HEAVEN AND EARTH

A tall fellow with salty hair
wanted to be a musician
but he was alone in the valley
with three accordions

The first accordion ended up rotting
In the simplicity of its soul
it would have liked to be a horse
but there was a lamp that burned
that kept burning

The second accordion trembled
like a house at its sister's footsteps
Thing is it was a big city
that was cheating on its residents
with its mayor
dumb as a crowbar

The third accordion
would have devoured the earth and the birds
if it had felt like it
But it was a sage
in the style of nettles
and contented itself envying motionless animals

But you will say to me
the gentleman who wanted to be a musician

He'd had time to die
and the leisure to smoke
and it was that smoke that rose from the earth to the clouds

A WATERSPOUT AT STARBOARD

LE CASQUE DE L'INCONNUE

Le vent la voix des insectes
caressent la joue du mélomane mourant
L'un d'eux plus grand que les autres
saute d'une illusion à l'autre
avec un rire muet
qui glace les os livides des déments
Ils sont mourants eux aussi
et ils rient parc que le rire est leur dernière cartouche
et qu'ils veulent tuer un soupir éternel
Mais ils meurent
et leur mort change l'ordre des désirs humains
Un jeune homme pâle
dont les yeux électriques sont les phares des forêts
recueille leur poussière
Il en enduit son front qui devient un canon épouvantable
dirigé contre la destinée de chacun

Et c'est fini
les nuages lassés du ciel sont tombés sur la terre
qui achève de cracher ses derniers animaux

THE HELMET OF THE UNKNOWN WOMAN

The wind the voice of insects
caress the cheek of the dying music lover
One of them bigger than the others
leaps from one illusion to another
with a mute laughter
that freezes the livid bones of the mad
They too are dying
and they laugh because laughter is their last shot
and because they want to kill an eternal sigh
But they're dead
and their death changes the order of human desires
A pale young man
whose electric eyes are lighthouses of the forests
gathers their dust
He coats his forehead with it which becomes a terrifying cannon
directed against the destiny of each one

And it's over
the clouds weary of the sky have fallen to earth
which finishes spitting out its last animals

JÉSUS DISAIT À SA BELLE-SŒUR

Nous avons fait le fumier
pour les fumières
l'évangile pour le crottin
et le malin pour la mâtine

En ce temps-là
la terre avait la forme d'une sabot de cheval
et le reste était à l'avenant
Les tapis précieux
paraient les arbres les plus nobles
et les maisons antiques
tourbillonnaient dans le soleil et la pluie
Alors une dame passa
et découvrit son ventre

JESUS SAID TO HIS SISTER-IN-LAW

We made crap
for the heaps
gospel for the sheep shit
and the devil for the vamp

In those days
the earth was shaped like a horse's hoof
and the rest followed accordingly
precious rugs
adorned the most noble trees
and antique houses
swirled up in the sun and rain
Then a woman passed by
and bared her belly

SAMSON

Or nous déléguées par les sceptres
traversions les plaines lustrées de l'arachnéenne chance
Aussi loin que les yeux les plus vils pouvaient contempler le triangle
    de sel
les poids du sommeil tombaient lourdement
Tombez poids
c'est grâce à vous que la nuit est plus blanche que l'ombre
et se revêt des robes ajourées de la montagne

Arrivez sources de ma main et réchauffez les ossements des glaciers
Arrivez sources de ma main et gelez les regards assombris
car tout regard qui s'assombrit
se plongera demain dans les révérences des miroirs
et les collines se cacheront sous les rendez-vous
C'est que les collines connaissent le langage des révérences
et savent la valeur des soupirs outremer
que poussent les longs cheveux blonds des *S*

Collines asseyez-vous sur le poids mort des lacs
car les larmes de vos pieds se perdent sur leurs bords
qui n'ont de limite que votre voix
si bouclée que s'y perdent les renards de vos oreilles
Ah si les collines voulaient se lier aux cygnes
que les nuages seraient rouges et promptes les floraisons
Hélas les collines s'en vont sur le chemin de sang
qui les mènera aux rocs de fumée et de torture
que protègent les mètres et les hôtels
Mais la colline n'est plus que le poteau du paysage
et le paysage n'est plus que le poteau de lui-même
Hé poteau Hé paysage Qu'attends-tu Voici le chien des pentes
Sois la vague et le bourreau la lance et l'orée
et que l'orée soit l'étincelle qui va du cou de l'amante à celui de l'amant

SAMPSON

So delegated by scepters
we crossed the glossy plains of arachnidean luck
As far as the vilest eyes could behold the triangle of salt
the weights of sleep fell heavily
Fall weights
thanks to you night is whiter than shadow
and clothes itself with the hemmed dresses of the mountain

Surge springs of my hand and rewarm the bones of glaciers
Surge springs of my hand and freeze darkened glances
because any glance that darkens
will plunge tomorrow into the reverences of mirrors
the hills will hide below the rendezvous
Indeed hills know the language of bows
and know the worth of overseas sighs
which shift the long blonde locks of the *S*

Hills go sit down on the dead weight of lakes
because the tears of your feet get lost on their banks
that have no limit but your voice
so curly that the foxes of your ears get lost there
Ah if the hills wanted to befriend the swans
how red the clouds would be and the flowerings quick
Alas the hills depart toward the path of blood
that will lead them toward rocks of smoke and torture
that meters and hotels protect
But the hill is no more than the post of the landscape
And the landscape is no more than the post of itself
Hey posts hey landscape What are you waiting for Here's the dog
    of hills
Be the wave and the hangman the spear and edge
and let the edge become the spark that goes from the neck of the
    beloved to that of the lover

et que se perde la lance dans la cervelle du temps
et que la vague porte la poutre
et que la poutre soit une hirondelle
blanche et rouge comme mon cœur et ma peur
Mais l'hirondelle ne sera jamais le paysage à fleur de peau
qui se cache comme le vent sur ton doigt séché
qui se roule en boule dans les tuyaux de la neige
Mais que le paysage découvre la caresse des collines
mordues par les étoiles
et les ponts s'ouvriront comme des oranges
Mais jamais les étoiles ne suivront le sillage des poissons étoilés
car leur mort est une question d'étoile
et les étoiles s'en iront désormais attaquer les bateaux
Bateaux vrilles feuilles onguents et chiffres
chiffres liqueurs visages pistes sourires bateaux et ail
pointes bateaux cheveux ours mon amour bateaux
conduisez la reine au port herbe tremblante qui coule comme une
    aiguille malgré son chas
conduisez la reine et son miroir
car la reine n'a pas de bateaux
la reine n'a pas d'aiguille
la reine n'a pas de miroir

and let the lance get lost in the brain of time
and let the wave carry the beam
and the beam become a swallow
white and red like my heart and my fear
But the swallow will never be the landscape skin deep
which hides itself like wind on your dried finger
which rolls as a ball in tubes of snow
But let the landscape discover the caress of hills bitten by stars
and bridges will open like oranges
But never will stars follow the wake of starry fish
because their death is a matter of star
and from now on the stars will depart to attack boats
Boats tendrils leaves salves and numbers
numbers liqueurs faces tracks smiles boats and garlic
points boats hair bears my love boats
Guide the queen to the port trembling grass that flows
    like a needle in spite of its eye
guide the queen and her mirror
because the queen has no boat
the queen has no needle
the queen has no mirror

LES BELLES MANIÈRES

A la lumière des cravates
on découvre les cœurs
et la saveur salée
des cheveux des servantes
Évente-toi si tu peux
le portier est aux hôtes
et les chats les chiens les cascades et les morts
Dans le port il y a un cerf malade
il a mangé des noix
Sa voix est chaude comme un astre
il regrette les autos des routes
et les poissons d'eau douce
Il a mangé des noix
des noix sans voix et sans chaleur
et sa peau se désole
comme une mine de charbon

GOOD MANNERS

By the light of neckties
one discovers hearts
and the salty flavor
of servants' hair
Fan yourself if you can
the doorman is at the hosts'
and the cats the dogs the waterfalls and the corpses
In the port there's a sick deer
he ate walnuts
His voice is warm like a star
he misses cars of the roads
and fish from fresh water
He ate walnuts
nuts without voice and without warmth
and his skin grieves
like a charcoal mine

LES JEUNES FILLES TORTURÉES

Près d'une maison de soleil et de cheveux blancs
une forêt se découvre des facultés de tendresse
et un esprit sceptique

Où est le voyageur demande-t-elle

Le voyager forêt se demande de quoi demain sera fait
Il est malade et nu
Il demande des pastilles et on lui apporte des herbes folles
Il est célèbre comme la mécanique
Il demande son chien
et c'est un assassin qui vient venger une offense

La main de l'un est sur l'épaule de l'autre

C'est ici qu'intervient l'angoisse une très belle femme en manteau de
   vison

Est-elle nue sous son manteau
Est-elle belle sous son manteau
Est-elle voluptueuse sous son manteau
Oui oui oui et oui
Elle est tout ce que vous voudrez
elle est le plaisir tout le plaisir l'unique plaisir
celui que les enfants attendent au bord de la forêt
celui que la forêt attend auprès de la maison

TORTURED YOUNG GIRLS

Near a house of sun and white hair
a forest discovers its gifts for tenderness
and a skeptical mind

Where is the traveler it asks

The forest traveler wonders what tomorrow will bring
He is sick and naked
He asks for lozenges and they bring him wild grass
He's famous as mechanical science
He calls for his dog
and it's an assassin that comes to avenge a wrong

One's hand is on the other's shoulder

Right here anguish intervenes a very beautiful woman in a mink coat

Is she naked under her coat
Is she pretty under her coat
Is she voluptuous under her coat
Yes yes yes and yes
She's everything that you could want
she's pleasure total pleasure rare pleasure
the one children await at the edge of the forest
the one the forest awaits near the house

AVENTURES D'UN ORTEIL

Sors de l'urne
dit l'hortensia à son complice
Et toi de ton Hortense lui répond la mandoline
qui n'était mandoline qu'à la faveur d'un rayon de soleil
ou d'une pièce de vingt sous tombée la nuit dans un ravin
La pièce de vingt sous se dresse comme une reine
et dit aux rochers dont les lèvres tremblent
Le grand crime aura lieu demain
mais il n'y a pas de crime sans chapeau
    il n'y a pas de crime sans étincelle
    il n'y a pas de crime sans potasse
    il n'y a pas de crime sans brebis
Et le grand crime n'aura pas lieu
car la terre est vide
les yeux se séparent de lunettes
et les ministres suppriment les corbillards
qui encombrent la voie lactée

ADVENTURES OF A TOE

Get out of the urn
says the hydrangea to its accomplice
And you get out of your Hortensia responds the mandolin
which was only a mandolin thanks to a sunbeam
or to a coin of twenty sous fallen at night in a ravine
The coin of twenty sous rises like a queen
and says to the boulders whose lips tremble
The big crime will take place tomorrow
but there's no crime without hat
    there's no crime without spark
    there's no crime without potash
    there's no crime without sheep
And the big crime will not take place
because the earth is empty
eyes separate themselves from glasses
and ministers suppress crows
who congest the milky way

RÉFORME

En traîneau sur la Néva
je glisse translucide
entouré d'hippocampes blancs
Petit cul pâle
que viens-tu faire ici
les casse-noisettes ont fermé leurs oreilles
les champignons poussent sur la fonte
Il n'y a plus que nous qui pensons aux gommes à effacer

REFORM

By sleigh over the Neva
I glide translucent
surrounded by white seahorses
Little pale ass
what're you doing here
nutcrackers have closed their ears
mushrooms grow on the thaw
We're the only ones left who think of gum erasers

SOUFFRE-DOULEURS

Robes courtes qui revenez
dites à l'essence des yeux
les détours sont inconnus au fond des nébuleuses
Les danses des métaux nus
jaillirent un matin du ventre d'un prélat
mais le calendrier accroupi sur le bateau
fiente dans la mer des jours décomposés
Des bancs de harengs saurs qui les avaient mangés
s'étalèrent en ligne de combat
et
    bouche à bouche nous nageons depuis les temps primaires

WHIPPING BOYS

Short dresses that come back
speak to the eye's essence
the detours are unknown in the depths of the nebulae
Dances of naked metals
spring one morning from the belly of a prelate
but the calendar crouched on the boat
droppings in the sea of decomposed days
Banks of kippers which have eaten them
spread out in a line of battle
and
    mouth to mouth we swim since primordial times

FLAMME BLEUE

L'heure du rendez-vous arrive sous la poterne avec quatre aiguilles en fibres de palmier. Avons-nous oublié les huit souvenirs que nous avons promis. Non l'oiseau du paradis s'est déplumé sur un front qui n'est pas le mien Quelle occasion pour perdre ce baiser Anis del oso pourquoi l'avez-vous teint Les soupirs de la chair fraîche ne sont pas pour la vieille mousse j'en appelle aux éventails que nous aimons pour leur cours limité par un bras de levier facilement mesurable Sur notre route des gouttes de sang coulant d'un vagin noir que nous voulons ignorer sont là pour nous reprocher d'avoir écrasé un papillon du soir sorti par l'une quelconque de nos narines

BLUE FLAME

The time of the rendez-vous occurs beneath the gate with four hands in fibers of palm. Have we forgotten the eight mementos that we promised. No the bird of paradise was plucked on a forehead not my own What chance to lose this kiss Anis del oso why did you dye it The sighs of fresh flesh are not for the old moss I appeal to the fans that we love for their span circumscribed by a lever arm easily measurable On our road drops of blood running from a dark vagina that we want to ignore are there to reproach us for having crushed a moth leaving by any one of our nostrils

LE PLUS LOINTAIN VISAGE

C'était un bras de fumée qui s'agitait comme un soleil
Mais si le soleil est plein comme une outre
le bras s'éloigne de l'avenue
tel le boiteux que poursuit une fourmi
Si le soleil est un pied d'enfant
espère La clavicule rougit dans sa gaîne
et la pomme s'envole vers l'hirondelle
Hélas l'hirondelle blanchit
sans se soucier du péril qui la menace
et la pomme usée comme un couteau d'amour
pleure en retournant aux fontaines noircies
Si le soleil s'ennuie dans son tombeau
nul époux ne caressera la route
nulle épouse ne secouera la pluie
mais sur la vierge ceinture de l'envolée
quelle main insensible signera *BARBICHE*
à l'heure où les eaux évadées de leurs prisons
diront au soleil mou
Tu es la barbiche et je suis le moineau

THE MOST DISTANT FACE

There was an arm of smoke that shook like a sun
But if the sun is full like a wineskin
the arm goes away from the avenue
like the lame chased by an ant
If the sun is a child's foot
hope The collarbone blushes in its sheath
and the apple flees toward the swallow
Alas the swallow pales
without worrying about the danger that threatens it
and the apple worn out like a knife of love
weeps in returning to the sullied fountains
If the sun grows bored in its tomb
no groom will caress the road
no bride will shake off the rain
but on the virgin belt of soaring
which insensitive hand will sign *GOATEE*
at the hour when waters escaping their prisons
will say to the soft sun
You're the goatee and I'm the sparrow

PIEDS ET POINGS LIÉS

Quand je serai le cheval de pierre
debout devant l'éternité
je demanderai aux divinités des plantes
le manteau de pluies indispensable aux voyageurs éternels
Aujourd'hui je suis dans le puits glacé
où pleurent les madones noyées par leurs larmes et la pluie éternelle
qui recouvre les pensées des hommes
leurs souvenirs et leurs ambitions déjà flétris
par une main inexperte
et incolore comme l'eau d'une carafe
où vit cependant l'œil de ma bien-aimée
couleur de citron et d'orage implacable

BOUND HANDS AND FEET

When I become the stone horse
standing before eternity
I will ask the gods of plants
for the coat of rains indispensable to eternal travelers
Today I am in the frozen well
where madonnas are crying drowned by their tears and eternal rain
that recovers the thoughts of men
their memories and their ambitions already deflated
by an unskilled hand
and colorless like the water of a carafe
where nevertheless the eye of my beloved lives
color of lemon and of unrelenting storm

MES DERNIERS MALHEURS

A Yves Tanguy.

270	Les bouleaux sont usés par les miroirs
441	Le jeune pape allume un cierge et se dévêt
905	Combien sont morts sur des charniers plus doux
1097	Les yeux du plus fort
	emportés par le dernier orage
1371	Les vieux ont peut-être interdit aux jeunes
	de gagner le désert
1436	Premier souvenir des femmes enceintes
1525	Le pied sommeille dans un bocal d'airain
1668	Le cœur dépouillé jusqu'à l'aorte
	se déplace de l'est à l'ouest
1793	Une carte regarde et attend
	Les dés
1800	Vernir il s'agit bien d'autre chose
1845	Caresser le menton et laver les seins
1870	Il neige dans l'estomac du diable
1900	Les enfants des invalides
	ont fait tailler leur barbe
1914	Vous trouverez du pétrole qui ne sera pas pour vous
1922	On brûle le *bottin* place de l'Opéra

MY LATE MISFORTUNES

to Yves Tanguy

270	The birches are worn out by mirrors
441	The young pope lights a candle and disrobes
905	How many corpses lie on the softest mass graves
1097	The eyes of the strongest carried off by the last storm
1371	The old may have forbidden the young to reach the desert
1436	First memory of pregnant women
1525	The foot dozes in a bronze jar
1668	The heart stripped to the aorta emigrates from east to west
1793	A map watches and waits for The dice
1800	Varnish surely it's about something else
1845	Caressing the chin and washing the breasts
1870	It snows in the devil's stomach
1900	Children of invalids had their beards trimmed
1914	You will find oil that's not for you
1922	We burn the phone book Place de l'Opéra

PORTRAIT D'ANDRÉ BRETON

Les gazelles ont caressé leur mémoire
Il en sort tout un équipage
avec de grandes dames sans yeux
un beau visage découvert
une voiture dont les oreilles écoutent écoutent écoutent et meurent
    d'ennui
L'ennui cultivé en des serres inestimables
se développe en capitaine de forbans
J'en suis

PORTRAIT OF ANDRÉ BRETON

The gazelles caressed their memory
Out of it comes a whole crew
with fine eyeless ladies
a handsome bare face
a car whose ears listen listen listen and die of boredom
Boredom cultivated in priceless greenhouses
develops into a pirate captain
I'm on board

PORTRAIT DE PAUL ELUARD

Les dents sombres montent sur les étoiles
Quelles étoiles
Une voix éclate sur le gazon meurtri
comme une fesse
Quelles fesses
Le vent couvre les cheveux des semences
Les semences passeront
mais tes nuages ne passeront pas
J'en ai un dans ma poche
qui s'élèvera jusqu'à ma bouche
alors je sourirai à tes étoiles

C'est gai hein

PORTRAIT OF PAUL ELUARD

Gloomy teeth climb on the stars
What stars
A voice explodes on the bruised lawn
like an ass
What asses
The wind covers the seeds' hair
The seeds will pass
but your clouds will not
I have one in my pocket
that will rise to my mouth
then I'll smile at your stars

That's cool eh

PORTRAIT DE GALA ELUARD

Il y a dans l'air un coup de revolver
tout seul
tant mieux
qui pleure
qui danse
et ainsi de suite
Il y a loin bien loin plus loin que tu ne penses
Une palme qui n'est pas dans une palmeraie
Une palmeraie où les animaux s'ennuient
ils t'attendent

PORTRAIT OF GALA ELUARD

In the air there's a gunshot
all alone
so much the better
that cries
that dances
and so on
There is far away quite far much farther than you think
A palm tree that's not in a grove
A grove where animals grow bored
they are waiting for you

PORTRAIT DE LOUIS ARAGON

Les bienfaits de la croissance
se constatent chaque jour
j'en suis témoin
et toi aussi
Maintenant tu as des mains dans les cheveux
et tes cheveux sont du verre
dont on fait les maréchaux
les capitaines au long cours
les cigares de luxe
et les wagons-lits

Bonjour mon petit

PORTRAIT OF LOUIS ARAGON

The benefits of growth
are noted each day
I'm a witness
and you too
Now you have some hands in your hair
and your hair is made of glass
from which they make marshals
the captains of long hauls
luxury cigars
and boxcars

Hello my pet

PORTRAIT DE MAX ERNST

Tes pieds sont loin
je les ai vus la dernière fois
sur le dos d'un cheval-jument
qui était mou qui était mou
trop mou pour être honnête
trop honnête pour être vrai

Le cheval le plus vrai
n'est jeune qu'un moment
mais toi
toi je te retrouve
dans les rues du ciel
dans les pattes des homards
dans les inventions sauvages

PORTRAIT OF MAX ERNST

Your feet are far away
I saw them the last time
on the back of a brood-mare
who was slow who was slow
too slow to be honest
too honest to be true

The truest horse
is young only a moment
but you
you I rediscover you
in heaven's streets
in the lobsters' claws
in wild inventions

PORTRAIT DE ROBERT DESNOS

La crème du rivage
a guéri tes battements de cœur

Salu-e

As-tu vu la liberté
Elle couche avec l'égalité
Vilaine va
Et si elle ne s'ennuie pas
nous lui donnerons
un petit serpent de mer
qui couvrira ses épaules
unies comme les États-Unis de la fraternité

PORTRAIT OF ROBERT DESNOS

The cream of the shore
has cured your heartbeats

Salut-e

Have you seen freedom
She sleeps with equality
Bad girl scat
And if she's not bored
we will give her
a little sea-serpent
that will cover her shoulders
unified like the United States of fraternity

LES YEUX DU VENT

La banlieue est bleue
quand passe le juge
Si le juge n'était pas juge
on verrait un phénomène
Quatre veaux
debout sur un paratonnerre
et criant
Liberté Liberté chérie
Et madame répondrait
Chéri
et monsieur
Bibi

THE WIND'S EYES

The suburb is blue
when the judge goes by
If the judge wasn't judge
you'd see a phenomenon
Four calves
standing on a lightning rod
and yelling
Liberty Liberty sweetie
And madame would reply
Darling
and mister
Me

LA CHUTE DES CORPS

J'ai un poil dans la tête
Il n'y en a pas autant dans la carafe
J'ai une mouche dans le nez
il y en a deux dans la calèche
Tournez tournez la roue
pour hisser les mendiants au sommet des cheminées
Les femmes le regarderont
les enfants le tueront
tournez tournez la roue
pour découper les Saint-Cyriens
Leur viande servira d'appât pour la pêche à Terre-Neuve
et l'année sera mauvaise
J'ai serré la main d'un idiot
et un myosotis pousse dans ma main
c'est qu'il fait chaud comme dans une conduite de gaz
où les hirondelles passent sans ses retourner
de crainte d'être changées en becs Auer
Que les raies du plancher zigzaguent dans leur ivresse
ou que les échelles s'effondrent sur ceux qui les bravent
le bruit de la rue sera lourd comme le sac d'un bagnard
les passants désolés se boucheront les oreilles
et les crises de nerfs de leurs épouses enceintes
détruiront l'équilibre des tables dans les chambres des hôtels

DOWNFALL OF THE BODIES

I have a hairbrain
There's even less in the carafe
I have a fly in my nose
there are two in the carriage
Turn turn the wheel
to hoist beggars to the top of chimneys
Women will look at it
children will kill it
Turn turn the wheel
to carve up the Saint-Cyriens
Their meat will act as bait for fishing in Newfoundland
and the year will be bad
I shook an idiot's hand
and a forget-me-not grows in my hand
thing is it's hot as in a gas pipe
where the swallows go without looking back
for fear of being changed into Auer lamps*
Let stripes of floorboard zigzag in their drunkenness
or ladders collapse on those that challenge them
street noise will be heavy like a convict's sack
distraught passersby will plug their ears
and the nervous breakdowns of their pregnant wives
will destroy the balance of the tables in hotel rooms

*Gas street lights invented in the late 19th century by a chemist, Carl Auer von Welsbach.

Petite vaisselle
aboutira
Beurre d'oiseau
grandira
Pelle de sel
patinera
Citron maudit
se mariera
Gazelle verte
s'éventera
Cigare de nuage
s'encaillera
Grande poussière
se développera
Manège de soie
dormira
Patère mélancolique
se balancera
Groseille fauve
flambera
Flamme solide
tressaillera
Carte à oreilles
bourgeonnera

Mais le jeune explorateur qui les mains vides franchit l'enceinte où le premier né les pieds joints le cœur avide et la cervelle cousue ravive l'incident lointain qui rendit impossible l'élection de la meule souveraine

Ainsi elle se pose jambes en l'air épaules lointain et mains partout mains multipliées par le détour et le roman découvert sous le chapeau

On bout on trempe dans la rue comme dans un baquet d'acide on se gonfle comme une aubergine on s'assoupit comme une bûche qui brûle on se meuble comme une cuvette Alors le marbre glisse le long des jambes mortes et s'étale sur l'équateur comme une petite flaque sonore

BLOOD AND ARRESTS

Little dish
will wind up
Bird's butter
will grow
Salt shovel
will skate
Cursed lemon
will marry
Green gazelle
will go flat
Cigar cloud
will go slumming
Huge dust
will develop
Silk carousel
will sleep
Melancholy coat hook
will sway
Tan currant
will ignite
Solid flame
will quiver
Map with ears
will sprout

But the young explorer who empty-handed escapes the compound where joined firstborn feet eager heart and sewn brain revive the distant incident that makes impossible the election of the sovereign millstone

So she puts legs in the air shoulders faraway and hands everywhere hands multiplied by the detour and the novel revealed beneath the hat

We boil we soak in the street as in a bucket of acid we inflate like an eggplant we swell like a burning log everyone furnishes themselves like a washbasin Then marble glides along dead limbs and stretches on the equator like a sonorous little puddle

UN MALHEUR NE VIENT JAMAIS SEUL

Les grues sont tombées sur l'amiante
avec leurs mains de poutres
gonflées de gaz étoilés
Un peu plus nous étions seuls
et c'eût été dommage
un lendemain de fête
Ce n'est pourtant pas gai
Une fête non plus
mais Jeanne d'Arc est heureusement morte
et les péniches coulées font l'amour avec elle
Un amour de cheval
qui ferait rire un Turc
A bas les moineaux

ONE MISFORTUNE NEVER COMES ALONE

The cranes have fallen on asbestos
with their hands of beams
swollen with starry gas
A close call we would have been alone
and it would have been a shame
a day after a holiday
It's not cheerful however
A holiday no more
but Joan of Arc is happily dead
and the sinking barges make love to her
A love of horse
which would make a Turk laugh
Down with sparrows

LES ENFANTS RIENT MAIS QUE FONT LEURS PARENTS

Souple corvette de mon cœur
l'acide te dévore
Faute de veau on fauche le foin
mais
souple corvette de mon cœur
ménage le sel
le sel te dévore
Souple corvette de mon cœur
prends garde
on construit des maisons
un peu partout
sur le sable des moulins
sur le ventre des femmes
et les enfants naissent
sous les yeux des tortues
Prends garde
souple corvette de mon cœur
voici l'époque de la moisson

CHILDREN LAUGH BUT WHAT DO THEIR PARENTS DO

Supple sloop of my heart
acid devours you
Lacking a calf one makes hay
but
supple sloop of my heart
ration salt
salt devours you
Supple sloop of my heart
take care
houses are built
nearly everywhere
on the sand of mills
on the bellies of women
and children are born
beneath the gaze of tortoises
Take care
supple sloop of my heart
here comes the era of the harvest

A UN VIRAGE EN *S*

La jeune femme
assise
sur les grandes neiges de je ne sais pas quoi
découvre le plus simple courage
s'enveloppe d'un manteau de pieds
léger comme un chapeau d'été
Un carillon hollandais
à la place de son sexe
capte les dernières rumeurs de la ville
Si elle mourait
les premières pudeurs du berger
tomberaient sur l'étang
qui en serait sali
et le cortège des sourds et des débiles
rongerait les derniers éléments

TO A BEND IN *S*

The young woman
seated
on the great snows of whatever
discovers the simplest courage
wraps herself with a foot blanket
light like a summer hat
A Dutch chime
in place of her sex
catches the last murmurs of the city
If she was dying
the first modesties of the shepherd
would fall on the pond
which would be soiled by them
and the procession of the deaf and dumb
would erode the last elements

NUAGE

Tombe pain d'épices
les blessés sont loin
les plantes sont mortes
et les malades respirent à peine

CLOUD

Let gingerbread fall
the wounded are distant
the plants are dead
and the sick hardly breathe

LA SEMAINE PÂLE

Blonde blonde
était la femme disparue entre les pavés
si légers qu'on les aurait cru de feuilles
si grands qu'on eût dit des maisons

C'était je m'en souviens un lundi
jour où le savon fait pleurer les astronomes

Le mardi je la revis
semblable à un journal déplié
flottant aux vents de l'Olympe
Après un sourire qui fila comme une lampe
elle salua sa sœur la fontaine
et retourna dans son château

Mercredi nue blême et ceinte de roses
elle passa comme un mouchoir
sans regarder les ombres de ses semblables
qui s'étendaient comme la mer

Jeudi je ne vis que ses yeux
signaux toujours ouverts pour toutes les catastrophes
L'un disparut derrière quelque cervelle
et l'autre fut avalé par un savon

Vendredi quand on aime
est le jour des désirs
Mais elle s'éloigna en criant
Tilbury tilbury ma flûte est perdue
Va-t'en la rechercher sous la neige ou dans la mer

THE PALE WEEK

Blonde blonde
was the woman disappearing amid the cobblestones
so light that one would have thought them leaves
so big that one would have said houses

It was I remember a Monday
day when the soap makes astronomers cry

That Tuesday I saw her again
similar to an unfolded newspaper
floating on the winds of Olympus
After a smile that went poof like a lamp
she waved to her sister the fountain
and reentered her chateau

Wednesday nude pale and cinched with roses
she passed by like a handkerchief
without noticing the shadows of her peers
which spread out like the sea

Thursday I only saw her eyes
signals always open for every catastrophe
One disappeared in back of some brain
and the other was swallowed by a soap

Friday when one loves
is the day of desires
But she distanced herself screaming
Tilbury tilbury my flute is lost
Go find it under the snow or in the sea

Samedi j'l'attendais une racine à la main
prêt à brûler en son honneur
les astres et la nuit qui me séparaient d'elle
mais elle était perdue comme sa flûte
comme un jour sans amour

Et j'attendais dimanche
mais dimanche ne vint jamais
et je restai dans le fond de la cheminée
comme un arbre égaré

Saturday I waited for her a root in my hand
ready to burn in her honor
the stars and the night which separated me from her
but she was lost like her flute
like a day without love

And I waited for Sunday
but Sunday never came
and I stayed in the hollow of the chimney
like a lost tree

LE COURAGE DU SERPENT

Ainsi sont mortes les nervures
Après avoir été
boxeurs peintres yachtmen
Elles étaient bien solides et bien tristes
les nervures
et mentaient comme un seul homme
l'homme aux bretelles
qui vit dans les solitudes
semées de balais
et de sculptures anciennes
Un jour elles oublièrent
et le mal se greffa
sur leur plus beau cartilage
c'était écrit
Le plus beau cartilage soupira
et se colla sur leur menton
Nom de dieu

THE SERPENT'S COURAGE

So the veins are dead
After having been
boxers painters yachtsmen
They were very solid and very sad
the veins
and they lied like a single guy
the man in suspenders
Who lives in solitudes
sown with brooms
and ancient sculptures
One day they will forget
and evil will be grafted
onto their most beautiful cartilage
It was written
The most beautiful cartilage will sigh
and will stick to their chin
God damn

VILLAGE SENTIMENTAL

40 découvertes pour 40 orteils
1 orteil par découverte
1 catastrophe par souvenir
1 conseil par côtelette
Tout cela pour le bonheur d'un rajah
un rajah somnolent
amateur de moutarde
inconnu du papier et voleur de savon

Il a vendu la chemise
du centenaire de Pasteur

SENTIMENTAL VILLAGE

40 discoveries for 40 toes
1 toe per discovery
1 catastrophe per memory
1 consult per cutlet
All that for the delight of a rajah
a sleepy rajah
amateur of mustard
undocumented and thief of soap

He sold the shirt
of the centenarian of Pasteur

DEVENUE VIEUX LE DIABLE SE FAIT ERMITE

Louis-Philippe est grand pour son âge
Donne-lui quelques sous
son chapeau sera trop petit
Donne-lui deux cravates
il mentira tous les jours
Donne-lui une autre pipe
sa mère pleurera
Donne-lui une paire de gants
il perdra ses chaussures
Donne-lui du café
il aura des ampoules
Donne-lui un corset
il portera un collier
Donne-lui des bretelles
il soignera des souris
Donne-lui un battoir
il montera en avion
Donne-lui un potage
il en fera une statue
Donne-lui des lacets
il mangera des groseilles

C'est Monsieur Louis-Philippe
qui vit de pilules et de buvards
mange sa mère
et perd l'heure en marchant

GROWN OLD THE DEVIL BECOMES A HERMIT

Louis-Phillipe is tall for his age
Give him some pennies
his cap will be too small
Give him two neckties
he'll lie every day
Give him another pipe
his mother will cry
Give him a pair of gloves
he'll lose his shoes
Give him coffee
he'll have blisters
Give him a corset
he'll wear a collar
Give him suspenders
he'll heal mice
Give him a club
he'll board a plane
Give him a soup
he'll make a statue of it
Give him shoelaces
he'll eat gooseberries

It's Monsieur Phillipe
who lives on pills and blotting-paper
eats his mother
and forgets time walking

MA MAIN DANS LA BIÈRE

A Jacques Prévert.

Le pendu est un pirate
qui avait des dents
qui avait des os
qui avait des os
avec de l'eau dedans

Puis il courut comme un serpent
sa mâchoire se détendit
sa langue monta sur son œil
Alors les sauterelles et les oignons
les bananes et les colliers
sortirent de sa poche un à un
Bonheur bonheur disaient-ils
sa bouche est la sœur de ma bouche
et il fait bon marcher dans la rue des Anesses

MY HAND IN THE BEER

To Jacques Prévert

The hanged man is a pirate
who had teeth
who had bones
who had bones
with water inside

Then he ran like a serpent
his moustache drooped
his tongue climbed up on his eye
Then the grasshoppers and the onions
bananas and necklaces
left his pocket one by one
Happiness Happiness they said
his mouth is the sister of my mouth
and it feels good to walk in the street of She-asses

LE DERNIER DON JUAN DE LA NUIT

Le quarante-deuxième pose son urine sur le canapé
Dansez voltigez les biroutes
Dépêche-toi j'ai envie de dormir

EDMOND ROSTAND

THE LAST DON JUAN OF THE NIGHT

The forty-second sets his piss on the couch
Dance dangle the dicks
Hurry up I want to sleep

EDMOND ROSTAND

SIMPLEMENT

A Marcel Duhamel.

Son cul sur son épaule
la tête basse les yeux en l'air
il parcourt le monde
et fume sa pipe à l'envers
O jours sans demi-lune
cirages fromages cartonnages
que faites-vous des animaux inférieurs

Les œufs aux aigrettes de soie
sèment des lacs d'encre bleue
guident sa mémoire

L'âme faible la chair forte le cul léger
il vole avec les papillons
la queue en l'air

SIMPLY

To Marcel Duhamel

His ass on his shoulder
head low eyes raised
he travels through the world
and smokes his pipe upside down
Oh days without half-moon
polishes cheeses cartons
what do you make of the inferior animals

The eggs of silk egrets
sow blue ink lakes
guide his memory

The weak soul the strong flesh the light ass
he flies with the butterflies
tail in the air

DEUX PETITES MAINS

Sur le cœur de la rue en gouttes d'eau
les bananes brodent des épingles
cuvent des orties
La robe de sang de la danseuse
tombe sur les pieds
du monsieur son amant
qui rit et qui s' efforce
qui s'efforce de couper un arbre
avec des dents de poissons
une échelle sur la jambe
C'est le pape

TWO LITTLE HANDS

On the heart of the street made of droplets
bananas embroider safety pins
ferment nettles
The dancer's dress of blood
falls at the feet
of mister her lover
who laughs and who strives
who strives to cut a tree
with fish teeth
a ladder on his leg
It's the pope

AS DE PIQUE

Je veux voir les choses éternelles qui fleurissent comme les cigarettes
que je fume dans la nostalgie de atlas de dix ans La symétrie des
châteaux intérieurs se divulgue aux regards des explorateurs blancs
J'irai à tâtons dans la chambre pleine de girafes chercher le manuscrit
que j'ai composé avec des morceaux de cervelle fraîche achetés au rabais
Parmi les musiciens que je connais, j'ai vu un jeune homme qui savait
les thèmes des symphonies d'aérolites.

Les camions automobiles et les grues respectueuses des quais annon-
cent Demain vaudra un jour de l'heure

> Le boulangers vous disent que c'est faux
> Mais les acteurs supputent les bravos

J'arriverai pour déjeuner en 1919

Auras-tu la tête neuve

Celle qui est jeune sait bien que c'est demain

Alors laissez-moi avoir le désir de quelques meurtres dans les
descentes solennelles des ascenseurs Ne me dites pas non les alcools
pourront peut-être me vieillir de quelques jours Je verrai des incendies
fastueux Celui de Rome était-il beau Une botte de paille Enlever la
croûte terrestre comme celle d'un pâté Je vous accrocherai pour vous
descendre dans un bain de feux-follets Un bâton dans la bouche vous
fera sourire Je ne veux pas de l'eau qui fait oublier Mes instants futurs
sont des chênes du Japon Autant de gestes que de microbes dans une
goutte d'eau Le vent le cœur humain la colonne de mercure Inusable
tout cela

Le cœur sur la main et la main sur le sein gauche

ACE OF SPADES

I want to see eternal things which flower like the cigarettes I smoke in nostalgia for the atlases of ten years old The symmetry of the internal castles divulges itself to the gazes of white explorers I will grope along in the room full of giraffes to look for the manuscript I composed with pieces of fresh brain bought cheaply Among the musicians that I know, I saw a young man who knew the themes of symphonies of meteors.

The trucks autos and law-abiding cranes of the docks announce Tomorrow will be worth a day of time

> The bakers tell you it's false
> But actors calculate the bravos

I'll arrive for lunch in 1919.

Will you have a new head

That woman who's young knows well that it's tomorrow

So let me have the desire for a few murders in the grave descents of the elevators Don't tell me no the drinks would perhaps age me by a few days I will see sumptuous fires That one from Rome was he handsome A bale of straw To lift the earthly crust like that of a pâté I will hang you to lower you into a bath of will-of-the-wisps A stick in your mouth will make you smile I do not want the water of forgetting My future moments are Japanese oaks As many gestures as microbes in a drop of water The wind the human heart the column of mercury Inexhaustible all that

The big-hearted hand and the hand on the left breast

Les crottes vertes sont tombées
Et changées en crottes jaunes
Il n'y a plus que des mains de Chinois
qui recherchent leurs poignets
sur le sol et dans nous-mêmes

Mais les moignons cachés au fond des poches
Les feront courir jusqu'à la fin de l'hiver

Il y a des toiles d'araignée partout Très bon pour les plaies cela dit-
on mais les fossés sont bordés d'épines où germent des baies noires J'en
ferai de l'encre et j'écrirai sur la poussière de la route

TOUTES LES ÉTOILES SONT AU GIBET DEPUIS LA MORT DES
PLÉSIOSAURES

Et personne ne passera plus sur la route parce que les lettres seront
des mitrailleuses hystériques Je partirai à cheval sure des cerveaux d'al-
iénés Et si je ne vois personne je ferai des alligators avec tous les ani-
maux du chemin Je traînerai ma troupe en larmes vers les cités paisibles
et sur leur passage ce sera l'ère des grands cataclysmes Si je vais sur
l'océan je charmerai tous les poissons et les pêcheurs me maudiront car
les poissons seront centenaires pour avoir fait trois fois le tour du globe

Je partirai Sept lieues d'un coup de pédale

Un grand bock d'espace s'il vous plaît
Anguille de route à rouler dans l'estomac

Poteaux indicateurs vous êtes des éventails
Il faut franchir des kilomètres morts

Tous ceux que tu as tués
viendront dans ton sommeil
te jeter du haut du ciel de lit
leur tête sur les jambes en 1919

The green droppings have fallen
And have changed into yellow droppings
What's left just Chinese hands
which look for their wrists
on the ground and within us

But the stumps hidden in the depths of pockets
Will make them run until the end of winter

There are spiderwebs everywhere Very good for the wounds it is
said but the pits are lined with thorns which sprout from the black
berries I will make ink from them and will write on the dust of the road

ALL THE STARS ARE ON THE GALLOWS SINCE THE DEATH OF THE
   PLESIOSAURS

And no one will go by on the road anymore because the letters will
be hysterical machine guns I will leave riding the brains of the mad And
if I see no one I will make alligators with all the animals of the road I
will drag my troops in tears toward the peaceful cities and on their path
this will be the era of great cataclysms If I go on the ocean I will charm
all the fish and the fishermen will curse me because the fish will be
hundred-year-olds from having three times circled the globe

I will go Seven leagues with one step on the pedal

A great beer mug of space if you please
Eel of road to roll in the belly

Guideposts you are fans
One must cover dead kilometers

All those you killed
will come in your sleep
throw you from the top of your bed
their head on legs in 1919

Et Demain

DEMAIN
Jamais les oiseaux verts ne seront des oiseaux rouges
Jadis
   Un citron dégorgeait des châteaux en Espagne
   Que mon docteur montait en bateaux plats
   Pourtant je préférais une souris

   Je changerai les métaux prisonniers des formes Et si quelqu'un dans ma prison me donne une figure de chien méchant j'aurai les flammes du foyer dans les yeux Les orgues des roues déroulent des écheveaux d'opéras Je les débrouillerai pour les chanter dans l'allégresse

Les amourettes des bouteilles d'encre et des porte-plumes
Baromètres ennemis des lois
Sans lois
Et vive le vagabondage spécial

   A ma voix les étoiles se jetteront dans les eaux noires On en retrouvera cachées au fond des puits et l'on reconnaîtra les temps prédits Si les yeux d'une femme inconnue cherchent à savoir ce qui sort des doigts du hasard tu lui opposeras des miracles inattendus La joie comme la peine se mesurent au centigramme Je connais la balance

Comme une poire

Un tatouage sur la main

J'affirme qu'un suicide est plus beau qu'un traité de paix.
Je joue aux dés
Ma vie ou ce château que n'est pas né
Taisez-vous le fusil est un oiseau des îles
Apprendrai-je à chanter ma victoire inutile parce que le
désir ne fait pas de miracles

And Tomorrow

TOMORROW
Never will green birds be red birds
Formerly
> A lemon spit out pipedream castles in Spain
> That my doctor mounted on flat-bottomed boats
> However I would prefer a mouse

I will transmute metals prisoners of forms And if someone in my prison makes a mean-dog face at me I will have the hearth's flames in my eyes The pipe organs of the streets unroll the skeins of the operas I will untangle them to sing them with joy

The fleeting affairs of bottles of ink and of penholders
Barometers enemies of the laws
Without laws
And long live the special vagrancy

At my voice the stars will throw themselves in black waters We will find them in the depths of wells and there we will recognize the predicted time If the eyes of an unknown woman seeking to know that which surges from the fingers of chance you will oppose her with unexpected miracles Joy like pain is measured by the centigram I know the balance

Like a pear

A tattoo on the hand

I affirm that a suicide is more beautiful than a peace treaty
I play at dice
My life or this castle that is not born
Shut up the gun is an island bird
Will I learn to sing my useless victory because
desire does not make miracles

Une pendule qui hésite entre minuit et une heure du matin heure des becs de gaz infatués de leur éclat volé aux cadrans solaires Vivre la vie impersonnelle des sèves et des minéraux Avant je veux qu'une femme que je n'ai jamais vue remue du doigt l'eau immobile d'un aquarium pour que les poissons croient à la fin du monde Un coup de revolver comme un salut Monsieur les plateaux sont parallèles au niveau de la mer. On m'évente avec des plumes de paon Quels yeux Du mercure dans un dé à coudre

Deux lampes dans un grenier vide
ou bien
          des airs mangés par les souris
Rien les lampes sont noyées dans la cave

J'aime les séjours dans les vitres verdâtres on fait des rencontres insoupçonnées Manières de comédie La poignée de mains du bull de la cour m'est moins agréable qu'une grosse émotion enroulée autour du bras. Une piqûre de moustique est un billet pour le palais des Glaces A chaque coup de pied je suis frappé dans la poitrine Pour la dernière il faut se servir des bras Il est difficile de revenir sur ses pas comme les tramways jusqu'à 1 2   1 1 1 1 1 1 1   2 2 2 2

ASSEZ

124

A pendulum that hesitates between midnight and one o'clock in the morning time of gas lamps infatuated by their gleam stolen from sundials To live the impersonal life of saps and minerals Before I want a woman that I have never seen to stir with her finger the motionless water of an aquarium so that fish believe in the end of the world A gunshot like a salute Mister the plateaux are parallel to sea level. I'm fanned with peacock feathers What eyes Of mercury in a thimble

Two lamps in an empty attic
or rather
        the airs eaten by mice
Nothing the lamps are drowned in the cellar

I love the visits in the greenish windowpanes we make unexpected encounters Manners of comedy The handshakes of the court bull are less agreeable to me than a hearty emotion wrapped with an arm. A mosquito bite is a ticket to the Palais des Glaces With each footfall I am stricken in the chest For the last woman it's necessary to use your arms It is difficult to return in her footsteps like the streetcars up to 1 2 1 1 1 1 1 1 2 2 2 2

    ENOUGH

MÉMOIRES DE BENJAMIN PÉRET

A Marcel Noll.

Un ours mangeait des seins
Le canapé mangé l'ours cracha des seins
Des seins sortit une vache
La vache pissa des chats
Les chats firent une échelle
La vache gravit l'échelle
Les chats gravirent l'échelle
En haut l'échelle se brisa
L'échelle devint un gros facteur
La vache tomba en cour d'assises
Les chats jouèrent la Madelon
et le reste fit un journal pour les demoiselles enceintes

THE MEMOIRS OF BENJAMIN PÉRET

A Marcel Noll

A bear ate the breasts
The sofa eaten the bear spat the breasts
From the breasts a cow came out
The cow pissed cats
The cats made a ladder
The cow climbed the ladder
The cats climbed the ladder
Up top the ladder broke
The ladder became a fat mailman
The cow fell into criminal court
The cats played *La Madelon*
and the rest went into a newspaper for unwed mothers.

LE QUATRIÈME DANSEUR

A Roland Iual.

Comme il dansait dans son pantalon
Un œuf sortit de la cuisine
à pas lents
comme une étoile un photographe
Jusqu'au lendemain il sortit
Jusqu'au lendemain il dansa
avec un collier
avec une musette
et la barbe lui poussa
tout au long de son pantalon
tout autour de la cuisine autour de la cuisine
qui n'est peut-être pas née

THE FOURTH DANCER

To Roland Iual

As it was dancing in its pants
An egg came out of the kitchen
with slow steps
like a star a photographer
Until the next day it came out
Until the next day it danced
with a collar
with a satchel
and its beard grew
all down the length of its pants
all around the kitchen around the kitchen
which perhaps was not born

LA MORT DU CYGNE

A R.G.

Un sexe sur un drapeau
peau peau peau de tes fesses
trottait comme un lapin
pin pin pin de hibou
du soir jusqu'au matin d'été
té té té téléphone au bon dieu
Mais l'été est funeste aux hiboux
Les hiboux du bon dieu
n'ont pas de fesses
pas de fesses et pas de malheurs
Ils vivent avec les lapins
et les bas de laine
l'été
L'été les fesses sont pâles
à cause des malheurs des hiboux
Les hiboux sans cervelle
trottent sur les drapeaux
et déchirent des sexes
Un sexe déchiré
c'est une croix désirée
Un drapeau sans sexe
est une pauvre moustache
Pauvre comme un hibou sans fesses

130

THE DEATH OF THE SWAN

To R.G.

A sex on a flag
skin skin skin of your asses
scurried like a rabbit
pine pine pine of owl
from evening until summer morning
tel tel tel telephone to good god
But summer is deadly to the owls
The owls of the good god
do not have asses
no asses and no sorrows
They live with the rabbits
and the wool stockings
summer
Summer the asses are pale
because of the sorrows of owls
The owls without brains
scurry over the flags
and tear the sexes
A torn sex
that's the desired cross
A flag without sex
is a poor moustache
Poor like an assless owl

A NOUS DEUX

A Janine Kahn.

Il s'appelait Villiod
D'une main il caressait la route
et de l'autre il tourmentait la mer

Drôle de quidam
que celui dont l'œil fermé
semblait toujours attendre la lune

Un matin il dansait sur une palme
et chantait Je suis celui que tu hais
regarde la forêt

La forêt comme un œil nu
attendait que mousse le vin
et il voulut ouvrir un bec

Le bec cria *Cocorico*
et Villiod mourut dans un salon

TO US TWO

To Janine Kahn

He was named Villiod
With one hand he caressed the road
and with the other he tormented the sea

Odd sort of fellow
that one whose closed eye
seemed always to reach the moon

One morning he was dancing on a palm
and was singing I am the one that you hate
look at the forest

The forest like a naked eye
waited for the wine to foam
and it wanted to open a beak

The beak cried *Cock-a-doodle-doo*
and Villiod died in a sitting room

LA FEMME À CHOSE

Saint-Raphaël se promène en souliers de paille
un quinquina dans les narines
un quinquina avec une cravate
une cigarette sur sa main
Sa main devient un tonneau
Un chien dans les environs
Il part avec les comestibles
C'est son affaire

THE WOMAN THING

Saint Raphael walks in shoes of straw
a quinine bark in his nostrils
a quinine bark with a tie
a cigarette on his hand
His hand becomes a barrel
A dog in the neighborhood
He leaves with the food
That's his business

VOYAGE DE DÉCOUVERTE

It était seul
dans le bas du seul-seul
Un seul à la seule
il seulait
Ça fait deux seuls
deux seuls dans un bas-seul

Un bas-seul ne dure pas longtemps
mais c'est assez quand on est seul
dans le bas du seul-seul

VOYAGE OF DISCOVERY

He was alone
in the depths of alone-alone
A loner to her loner
he was going it alone
That makes two loners
two loners in a low-alone

A low-loner does not last long
but that's enough when one is alone
in the depths of alone-alone

26 POINTS À PRÉCISER

A André Masson.

Ma vie finira par a

Je suis $b\text{-}a$

Je demande $cb\text{-}a$

je pèse les jours de fête $\dfrac{d}{cb\text{-}a}$

Mes prévisions d'avenir $\dfrac{de}{cb\text{-}a}$

Mon suicide heureux $\dfrac{de}{(cb\text{-}a)f}$

Ma volonté $\sqrt[g]{\dfrac{de}{(cb\text{-}a)f}}$

Ma force physique $\sqrt[g]{\dfrac{de}{(cb\text{-}a)f}}\!+\!h$

Mes instincts sanguinaires $\sqrt[g]{\dfrac{de}{(cb\text{-}a)f}}\!+\!h\text{-}i$

Les cartes ont mis dans ma poche $\left(\sqrt[g]{\dfrac{de}{(cb\text{-}a)f}}\!+\!h\text{-}i\right)^{j}$

26 POINTS TO MAKE CLEAR

To André Masson

My life will end by a

I am $b\text{-}a$

I ask $cb\text{-}a$

I measure the holidays $\dfrac{d}{cb\text{-}a}$

My predictions for the future $\dfrac{de}{cb\text{-}a}$

My happy suicide $\dfrac{de}{(cb\text{-}a)f}$

My will $\sqrt[g]{\dfrac{de}{(cb\text{-}a)f}}$

My physical force $\sqrt[g]{\dfrac{de}{(cb\text{-}a)f}}+h$

My bloodthirsty instincts $\sqrt[g]{\dfrac{de}{(cb\text{-}a)f}}+h\text{-}i$

The cards placed in my pocket $\left(\sqrt[g]{\dfrac{de}{(cb\text{-}a)f}}+h\text{-}i\right)^{j}$

Elles ont retiré $\left(\sqrt[g]{\dfrac{de}{(cb-a)f}}+h-i\right)^{j}+k$

Il reste $\left(\sqrt[g]{\dfrac{de}{(cb-a)f}}+h-i\right)^{j}+kl$

Avec mon nez je sens $m\left(\sqrt[g]{\dfrac{de}{(cb-a)f}}+h-i\right)^{j}+kl$

Avec ma langue je dis $\dfrac{m}{n}\left(\sqrt[g]{\dfrac{de}{(cb-a)f}}+h-i\right)^{j}+kl$

Avec ma bouche je mange $\dfrac{m}{n}\left(\sqrt[g]{\dfrac{de}{(cb-a)f}}+h-i\right)^{j}+kl+o$

Avec mes yeux je vois $\dfrac{\dfrac{m}{n}\left(\sqrt[g]{\dfrac{de}{(cb-a)f}}+h-i\right)^{j}+kl+o}{p}$

Avec mes oreilles j'entends $\dfrac{\dfrac{m}{n}\left(\sqrt[g]{\dfrac{de}{(cb-a)f}}+h-i\right)^{j}+kl+o}{pq}$

They withdraw $\left(\sqrt[g]{\dfrac{de}{(cb-a)f}}+h-i\right)^{j}+k$

What remains $\left(\sqrt[g]{\dfrac{de}{(cb-a)f}}+h-i\right)^{j}+kl$

With my nose I smell $m\left(\sqrt[g]{\dfrac{de}{(cb-a)f}}+h-i\right)^{j}+kl$

With my tongue I speak $\dfrac{m}{n}\left(\sqrt[g]{\dfrac{de}{(cb-a)f}}+h-i\right)^{j}+kl$

With my mouth I eat $\dfrac{m}{n}\left(\sqrt[g]{\dfrac{de}{(cb-a)f}}+h-i\right)^{j}+kl+o$

With my eyes I see $\dfrac{\dfrac{m}{n}\left(\sqrt[g]{\dfrac{de}{(cb-a)f}}+h-i\right)^{j}+kl+o}{p}$

With my ears I hear $\dfrac{\dfrac{m}{n}\left(\sqrt[g]{\dfrac{de}{(cb-a)f}}+h-i\right)^{j}+kl+o}{pq}$

Avec mes mains je gifle
$$\frac{\dfrac{m}{n}\left(\sqrt[g]{\dfrac{de}{(cb-a)f}}+h-i\right)^{j}+kl+o}{pq+r}$$

Avec mes pieds j'écrase
$$\frac{\dfrac{m}{n}\left(\sqrt[g]{\dfrac{de}{(cb-a)f}}+h-i\right)^{j}+kl+o}{(pq+r)\,s}$$

Avec mon sexe je fais l'amour
$$\frac{\dfrac{m}{n}\left(\sqrt[g]{\dfrac{de}{(cb-a)f}}+h-i\right)^{j}+kl+o}{\sqrt[t]{(pq+r)\,s}}$$

La longueur de mes cheveux
$$\frac{\dfrac{m}{n}\left(\sqrt[g]{\dfrac{de}{(cb-a)f}}+h-i\right)^{j}+kl+o}{\sqrt[t]{(pq+r)\,s}}-u$$

Mon travail du matin
$$\frac{\dfrac{m}{n}\left(\sqrt[g]{\dfrac{de}{(cb-a)f}}+h-i\right)^{j}+kl+o}{\sqrt[t]{(pq+r)\,s}}-uv$$

Mon travail de l'après-midi
$$\frac{\dfrac{m}{n}\left(\sqrt[g]{\dfrac{de}{(cb-a)f}}+h-i\right)^{j}+kl+o}{\sqrt[t]{(pq+r)\,s}}-uv-w$$

142

With my hands I slap
$$\dfrac{\dfrac{m}{n}\left(\sqrt[g]{\dfrac{de}{(cb-a)f}}+h-i\right)^{j}+kl+o}{pq+r}$$

With my feet I crush
$$\dfrac{\dfrac{m}{n}\left(\sqrt[g]{\dfrac{de}{(cb-a)f}}+h-i\right)^{j}+kl+o}{(pq+r)\,s}$$

With my sex I make love
$$\dfrac{\dfrac{m}{n}\left(\sqrt[g]{\dfrac{de}{(cb-a)f}}+h-i\right)^{j}+kl+o}{\sqrt[t]{(pq+r)\,s}}$$

The length of my hair
$$\dfrac{\dfrac{m}{n}\left(\sqrt[g]{\dfrac{de}{(cb-a)f}}+h-i\right)^{j}+kl+o}{\sqrt[t]{(pq+r)\,s}}-u$$

My morning's work
$$\dfrac{\dfrac{m}{n}\left(\sqrt[g]{\dfrac{de}{(cb-a)f}}+h-i\right)^{j}+kl+o}{\sqrt[t]{(pq+r)\,s}}-uv$$

My afternoon's work
$$\dfrac{\dfrac{m}{n}\left(\sqrt[g]{\dfrac{de}{(cb-a)f}}+h-i\right)^{j}+kl+o}{\sqrt[t]{(pq+r)\,s}}-uv-w$$

Mon sommeil
$$\left(\dfrac{\dfrac{m}{n}\left(\sqrt[g]{\dfrac{de}{(cb-a)f}}+h\right)^{j}+kl+o}{\sqrt[t]{(pq+r)\,s}}-uv-w\right)^{x}$$

Ma fortune
$$\left(\dfrac{\dfrac{m}{n}\left(\sqrt[g]{\dfrac{de}{(cb-a)f}}+h\right)^{j}+kl+o}{\sqrt[t]{(pq+r)\,s}}-uv-w\right)^{x}-y$$

Ma date de naissance
$$\left(\dfrac{\dfrac{m}{n}\left(\sqrt[g]{\dfrac{de}{(cb-a)f}}+h\right)^{j}+kl+o}{\sqrt[t]{(pq+r)\,s}}-uv-w\right)^{x}-\dfrac{y}{z}$$

My sleep
$$\left(\dfrac{\dfrac{m}{n}\left(\sqrt[g]{\dfrac{de}{(cb-a)f}}+h\right)^{j}+kl+o}{\sqrt[t]{(pq+r)\,s}}-uv-w\right)^{x}$$

My fortune
$$\left(\dfrac{\dfrac{m}{n}\left(\sqrt[g]{\dfrac{de}{(cb-a)f}}+h\right)^{j}+kl+o}{\sqrt[t]{(pq+r)\,s}}-uv-w\right)^{x}-y$$

My date of birth
$$\left(\dfrac{\dfrac{m}{n}\left(\sqrt[g]{\dfrac{de}{(cb-a)f}}+h\right)^{j}+kl+o}{\sqrt[t]{(pq+r)\,s}}-uv-w\right)^{x}-\dfrac{y}{z}$$

LA GRAND MISÈRE DES DERNIERS CAILLOUX

A Simone Breton.

C'est qu'il découvrit l'Amérique et les jupons
les pancartes et les bonnes sœurs
C'est que toutes les migraines se soutiennent
autour de sa grandeur ensoleillée

Le président des achats vend le 13 pour le 15
use ses moustaches comme du verre
mange comme un chat
pisse comme un hôtel

A l'heure où le plus jeune carburateur
emploie ses derniers joncs
pour le dernier garçon
La femelle se cache dans un drapeau
autour d'un ventre
sous des lunettes

THE GREAT MISERY OF THE LAST STONES

To Simone Breton

Because he discovers America and the slips
the placards and the good sisters
Because all the migraines keep going
around his sunny grandeur

The president of sales sells number 13 for 15
uses his moustache like glass
eats like a cat
pisses like a hotel

At the hour when the youngest carburetor
uses its last lines
for the last boy
The female hides herself in a flag
around a stomach
under eyeglasses

LE (A) CÉLÈBRE CAVALIER (ÈRE)

Poule et poule
voici l'ampoule
qui sourit en pensant à Horace

Oh fille d'agave
oh pieds de coton
tu auras la vie sauve
car il te manque
un sexe frais pour être honnête
un cheveu pour être belle

Une pierre
et je penserai à toi
Un voyage
et je serai i' imbécile que tu sais
Et nous rirons bien quand même

THE (A) FAMOUS HORSEMAN (WOMAN)

Fowl and fowl
here's the vial
which smiles thinking of Horace

Oh daughter of agave
oh feet of cotton
your life will be spared
because you're missing
a fresh sex to be honest
a hair to be beautiful

A stone
and I will think of you
A journey
and I will be the imbecile that you know
And we will laugh hard even so

PAR LE TROU DE LA SERRURE

Lève la tête et fais le mort
Quand tu t'en iras les pieds devant
les barreaux de la cage auront des ailes légères
qui battront la charge dans la cave
et les souffles humides des tapis usés
balaieront lourdement les cris suspects des volailles
Minuit sonnant dans la cheminée déserte
comme un rat aventureux
ranimera le timide sourire des casquettes neuves
qui voyageant dans l'ombre
regardent passer près d'elles les persiennes closes
qui n'ont jamais songé aux malheurs des serpents accroupis devant les
    portes cochères
Ce sera la nui et peut-être le jour
Les grands arbres seront morts
et les seins suspendus à leurs branches
se soulèveront régulièrement pour signifier leur sommeil
Tu n'en seras pas dupe comme les lames du parquet
mais riras bien haut pour effrayer les balcons
hardes mal lavées qui sèchent sans espoir de sécher
comme on meurt
blessé au coin d'un bois
et surveillé par les grands papillons blancs
chemises des herbes
Tout cela tout cela parce qu'un chien court après sa queue
et ne la retrouve pas
parce que les pavés sont sortis en rangs pressés et menacent les rivières
parce que les plantes dépérissent dans des scaphandres désaffectés
parce que l'eau ne s'égoutte plus entre les doigts
tout cela enfin parce que tu n'es plus qu'une figurine
découpée dans un billet de banque

BY THE KEYHOLE

Lift your head and play dead
When you depart feet first
the bars of the cage will have light wings
which will sound the charge in the cellar
and the humid breaths of used rugs
will sweep away clumsily suspicious cries of poultry
Midnight sounding in the deserted fireplace
like an adventurous rat
will revive the timid smile of new caps
which traveling in the shadow
watch pass along near them closed shutters
that have never dreamed of the miseries of crouched serpents in front of
    the livery doors
It will be night and perhaps day
The tall trees will be dead
and breasts hanging from their branches
will rise up regularly to signify their sleep
You will not be fooled by that like the floorboards
but will laugh very loudly to scare off balconies
old clothes badly washed which dry without hope of drying
as one dies
wounded in the corner of a wood
and watched by the great white butterflies
shirts of grasses
All this all this because a dog runs after its tail
and does not find it
because the cobblestones are leaving in hurried ranks and menace the
    rivers
because the plants waste away in disaffected diving suits
because the water does not drip any more between the fingers
all this finally because you are no more than a figurine
cut out in a bank note

IL N'Y A QU'UNE MERVEILLE SUR LA TERRE

Je ne pense à dieu
qu'en mangeant du chiendent
parce que dieu
a fait le chiendent à son image
qui est un mouchoir
Il suffit d'une goutte d'eau
tombant d'un nuage aussi ancien que Jules César
pour que la glace se fende de haut en bas
comme une orange
laquelle est faite à l'image de ma sœur
Entre parenthèses
ma sœur ne prêche jamais la miséricorde divine
car elle est divine
divine te dis-je
divine comme une mouche sur un arbre de quatre-vingt-dix mètres de
    diamètre
divine comme une soucoupe de mica
divine comme un hippopotame de quatre siècles
divine comme un ivrogne sur le Mont-Blanc
divine comme moi
qui suis son frère de temps en temps
Un jour je te dirai
ce qu'il faut faire d'un serpent
Aujourd'hui
donne-le à une femme de vingt-cinq ans
blonde de préférence
et tu verras deux serpents
Donne les deux serpents à un curé
et tu verras le pape
mourir d'une fluxion de poitrine

THERE IS ONLY ONE MARVEL ON EARTH

I only think of god
when eating quackgrass
because god made
quackgrass in his image
which is a handkerchief
All it takes is one drop of water
falling from a cloud as ancient as Julius Caesar
for the mirror to crack from top to bottom
like an orange
which is made in the image of my sister
Between parentheses
my sister never preaches divine mercy
because she is divine
divine I'm telling you
divine like a fly on a tree ninety meters in diameter
divine like a saucer of mica
divine like a hippopotamus four centuries old
divine like a drunk on Mont Blanc
divine like me
who's her brother from time to time
One day I'll tell you
what you must do with a serpent
Today
give it to a twenty-five year old woman
preferably blonde
and you will see two serpents
Give the two serpents to a priest
and you will see the pope
die of chest congestion

LE LANGAGE DES SAINTS

Il est venu
il a pissé
comme il était seul
il est parti
mais il reviendra
l'œil dans la main
l'œil dans le ventre
et sentira
l'ail les aulx
Toujours seul
il mangera les asperges bleues des cérémonies officielles

THE LANGUAGE OF SAINTS

He came
he pissed
How alone he was
he left
but he'll come back
his eye in his hand
his eye in his belly
and he'll smell
garlic garlics
Always alone
he will eat the blue asparagus of official ceremonies

LES ENFANTS DU QUADRILATÈRE

A Jacques Baron.

Quand le soleil
descendra sur la terre avec sa moustache
nous ouvrirons les valises
et les fils des derniers rats
oublieront leur langage
Dans la chambre
les oranges rouleront jusqu'au soleil
Si quelqu'un demande l'heure
la dernière venue lui donnera sa bouche
comme un gant
et sans se souvenir de son père
lui dira qu'il n'y a pas de fleurs sans fumée
ni de pleurs sans colère
Ventre de ventre
mon ventre
ni pleurs sans colère

THE CHILDREN OF THE QUADRANGLE

To Jacques Baron

When the sun
sets on the earth with its moustache
we will open the luggage
and the sons of the last rats
will forget their language
In the room
the oranges will roll up to the sun
If someone asks the time
the last to arrive will give him her mouth
like a glove
and without remembering his father
will tell him that there are no flowers without smoke
nor tears without rage
Belly of belly
my belly
no tears without rage

VERS L'OUEST

Mieux vaut se coudre les mains
que de rire aux anges
Mieux vaut changer de montre
que de hurler à la lune

TOWARD THE WEST

Better to sew up your hands
than to roar with laughter
Better to change your watch
than to howl at the moon

BIENSÉANCE

La voiture était pleine d'eau
qui couvrait la mouture mangée par la monture
C'était un beau diamant
taillé en forme de voiture
C'était celle de la tortue

ETIQUETTE

The car was full of water
which covered the mash eaten by the mount
It was a beautiful diamond
cut in car shape
It was that of the turtle

LES CHEVEUX AU VENT

Accours du fond des troncs ô sable
pauvre sable des revenants
toi qui sauves les mains
et leurs attributs
Le sang cravaté de nuages
pour le plaisir des dames
pour le plaisir des orgues
botté crotté
n'a plus d'image
Il est presque nu
et son sourire
est fonction de la chaleur

THE WIND'S HAIR

Run from the bottom of the trunks oh sand
poor sand of ghosts
you who save hands
and their attributes
The necktied blood of clouds
for the pleasure of women
for the pleasure of church organs
muddy booted
has no more picture
It's almost naked
and its smile
depends on the heat

QUATRE ANS APRÈS LE CHIEN

A Pierre Unik.

Ici commence la maison glaciale
où la rotondité de la terre n'est plus qu'un mot
aussi léger qu'une feuille
dont la nature importe peu
Dans la maison glaciale danse
tout ce que le mouvement de la terre ne peut pas empêcher de danser
toute la vie impossible et souhaitée tant de fois
tous les êtres dont l'existence est improbable
Là le temps équivaut au partage d'un empire
à une longue marche de Lilliputiens
à une cataracte de 1800 mètres de hauteur

Passons aux actes
Une jeune femme entre dans la maison glaciale
fend un escalier dans toute sa longueur
et le couvre de fumier
un fumier d'étoiles rongé par des dollars
Elle passa sa main sur ses yeux
et *la Liberté éclairant le monde* est la place de l'escalier
Elle crie tempête jure
à tel point que l'air en est bouleversé

Les oiseaux nécrophages
qui sont peut-être des insectes
tombent du plafond
s'enfoncent dans le sol
et vont se fixer pour toute l'éternité
au centre de la terre
qui en est toute émue

C'est alors qu'apparaît la maladie du sommeil
Le sommeil des arbres excite les vagues lubriques

FOUR YEARS AFTER THE DOG

To Pierre Unik

Here the icy house begins
where the roundness of earth is no more than a word
as light as a leaf
whose nature matters little
In the icy house dances
all that which earth's movement cannot stop from dancing
all life impossible and yearned for so many times
all creatures whose existence is impossible
There time amounts to the splitting of an empire
to a long march of Lilliputians
to a waterfall 1800 meters high

Let's move on to the acts
A young woman enters the icy house
splits a staircase down its entire length
and covers it with manure
a shitheap of stars gnawed by dollars
She draws her hand over her eyes
And *Lady Liberty lighting up the world* is the place of the staircase
She cries storms swears
to such an extent that the air gets upset by it

Carrion birds
who may be insects
fall from the ceiling
sink into the ground
and go fasten themselves for all eternity
to the center of the earth
which is very touched by them

That's when the sleep disturbance appears
The sleep of the trees excites the lewd waves

et l'amour bondit comme un chien hors de sa niche
Autrement dit les vagues n'ont pas la force la foi qui soulève les
    montagnes
Je leur prête mon sexe et tout est dit
et nous sommes tous très satisfaits

Une heure plus tard je le serai moins
car je marcherai sur ma barbe

La maison glaciale s'est déplacée
comme un tremblement de terre
et un caractère énergique
voici qu'à la chaleur communicative des banquets
un nouvel aspect des montagnes
doit son existence à une impropriété de termes
Il n'en faut pas plus pour qu'un savant
un savant authentique à ce qu'on dit
crie au miracle
Dans toutes les classes de la société
on ne songe plus qu'à jouir avec tous ses organes
Un député qui joua un rôle dans l'Affaire
affirme qu'il jouit par les poumons
Je veux bien le croire
quant à moi je monte dans un arbre
qui porte la tour Eiffel dans son ombre
et dont les racines ont vomi le soldat inconnu
De là j'aperçois la maison glaciale
dans le bec d'une tourterelle
Est-ce la paix ou la guerre
Vite un taxi un aéroplane un cheval
Ca y est je suis arrivé
et mes jambes deviennent extraordinairement fortes
C'est qu'elles s'allongent outre mesure
Je suis un arbre immense qui couvre la terre de son ombre
Ah vous pouvez rigoler maintenant
vous n'êtes pas prêts de voir la lumière du soleil

and love leaps like a dog out of its kennel
In other words the waves do not have the force the faith that lifts
    mountains
I lend them my sex and all's said
and we are all very satisfied

An hour later I will be less so
because I'll step on my beard

The icy house moves
like an earthquake
and a forceful character
suddenly with the communicative warmth of banquets
a new aspect of the mountains
owes its existence to an impropriety of terms
It doesn't take much more until a wise man
an authentic wise man according to some
shouts a miracle
In all classes of society
no one dreams of anything but climaxing with all his organs
A deputy who played a role in The Affair
affirms that he comes with his lungs
I truly want to believe it
as for me I climb a tree
which bears the Eiffel Tower in its shadow
and whose roots have vomited the unknown soldier
From there I notice the icy house
in the beak of a turtledove
Is this peace or war
Quick a taxi an airplane a horse
That's it I've arrived
and my limbs are becoming extraordinarily strong
I mean they stretch beyond measure
I am an immense tree that covers the earth with its shadow
Ah you can giggle now
you are not close to seeing the sunlight

Le soleil est une éclipse qui dure toute une époque géologique
et les enfants de l'époque ne s'en rappellent pas la couleur
Ceux pour lesquels maison glaciale de leurs cheveux
est une chambre d'amour
ont le bonheur aux lèvres
mais lorsqu'ils perdent leurs lèvres
ils s'ennuient tellement
qu'ils envient la vie des insectes adultes
C'est alors que je passerai
un rocher dans les mains
attendant que l'oiseau de la résurrection
se pose lourdement sur mon épaule
La droite ou la gauche

The sun is an eclipse that lasts for an entire geological era
and the children of the era don't remember the color of it
Those for whom the icy house of their hair
is a bedroom for love
have happiness on their lips
but when they lose their lips
they're so distressed
that they envy the life of adult insects
That's when I pass by
a rock in my hands
waiting for the bird of the resurrection
to perch heavily on my shoulder
The right or the left

PARTIE DOUBLE

L'onagre de paille
pour la course à l'orage
se range devant les taxis de feutre

Le jockey
cerise molle et gutta-percha
pendule aux quatre coins
car il n'aime pas la pipe du majordome

Tout cela rend un son bizarre

DAILY DOUBLE

The donkey of straw
for the race to the storm
pulls over in front of the felt taxis

The jockey
cherry limp and rubbery
pendulum at the four corners
because he doesn't like the butler's pipe

All this makes a weird noise

PREUVE FORMELLE

Sais-tu mourir sans la permission du nageur
si tu réponds oui
tu es l'homme annoncé par la loi
l'audacieux aux lèvres d'éléphant
le menteur éprouvé par le fer et le feu
le savant démoniaque qui changera le monde en filet de sang
l'enfer de poix où tomberont les êtres miraculeux
que tu rencontres chaque soir en sortant du théâtre
mine de sel
avenue décorée de fleurs sauvages
orage sexuel
pour décourager les conquérants de la Grande Roue

FORMAL PROOF

Do you know how to die without permission of the swimmer
and if you answer yes
you are the man heralded by the law
the brazen one with elephant lips
the liar tested by steel and fire
the demonic sage who will change the world into a trickle of blood
the hell of pitch where miraculous beings will fall
that you meet each evening leaving the theatre
salt mine
avenue decorated with wild flowers
sexual storm
to discourage the conquerors of the Big Ferris Wheel

LE MARIAGE DES FEUILLES

L'homme découvre la poésie circulaire
Il s'aperçoit qu'elle roule et tangue
comme les flots de la botanique
et prépare périodiquement son flux et son reflux

O saints que n'êtes-vous ceints de seins sains
Votre seing figurerait une main de pouces
agitée d'un tremblement alcoolique
O saints qu'avez-vous sur la main
Est-ce une main plus petite
que recouvre une autre main plus petite
et ainsi jusqu'à la consommation des mains

La poussière s'agite dans sa solitude
Elle veut que le silence qui l'entoure
se peuple de fantômes ailés
aux voix de troncs pourris
de femmes légères comme la dame blanche
de vieillards descendus de la montagne
en proie aux neiges éternelles
des grandes montagnes molles
où tournent virent et plongent
les chaussons de danse

THE MARRIAGE OF LEAVES

Man discovers circular poetry
He notices that it rolls and pitches
like botanical waves
and prepares periodically its ebb and flow

Oh saints if only you were circled with healthy breasts
Your signature would draw a hand all thumbs
shaking with alcoholic tremors
Oh saints what's in your hand
Is it a smaller hand
that conceals another smaller hand
and so on until the consummation of hands

Dust tosses in solitude
It wants the silence that surrounds it
to be crowded with winged phantoms
with voices of rotten trunks
of women easy like snow white
of old men down from the mountains
gripped by eternal snows
of the great slack mountains
where dancing slippers
turn spin and plunge

AVEZ-VOUS DU WHISKY

Lente fumée bleue où s'attardent tes pas
mer sobre
Salut poisson d'évangile
toi qui naquis dans la main d'une voluptueuse
et mourus sous les regards d'un roi

La tombe s'ouvrira pour laisser passer une bannière
La bannière suivra la rive gauche du canal
jusqu'à la jambe humaine
qui sépare l'amour de la mort
Elle portera cette jambe sur le sommet de la montagne
qui cessera de cracher des glaïeuls
pour devenir un troupeau d'hermines

Et dans le ciel nocturne
peuplé de scolopendres
une barre de fer maniée par un sultan
broiera pendant l'éternité des têtes étincelantes

DO YOU HAVE ANY WHISKEY

Slow blue smoke where your steps linger
sober sea
Greetings fish of the gospel
you who were born in the hand of a voluptuous woman
and died beneath the gaze of a king

The tomb will open to allow a banner to pass by
The banner will follow the left bank of the canal
far as the human leg
which separates love from death
It will carry this leg on the summit of the mountain
and will stop spitting gladiolas
in order to become a pack of ermines

And in the night sky
peopled with centipedes
a steel pipe wielded by a sultan
will crush for eternity sparkling heads

HONOREZ VOS MORTS

A Raymond Queneau.

Dans la main
il y a la hache
dans la hache
il y a le chapeau la tête le cou les pieds
et le souvenir des intestins
Il y a aussi
le courage des petites lumières
qui ne craignent pas la contagion
Il y a encore un tremblement nerveux
C'est la contagion
et une pente abrupte
qui pourrait cacher des oies
mais elle n'en cache pas
car à droite
il y a une tache grasse
c'est de l'huile

HONOR YOUR DEAD

To Raymond Queneau

In your hand
there's a hatchet
in the hatchet
there's the hat head neck feet
and the memory of intestines
There's also
the courage of little lights
which do not fear contagion
There's still a nervous trembling
It's the contagion
and a steep slope
which could hide geese
but it does not hide them
because to the right
there's a grease stain
it's oil

MYSTÈRE DE MA NAISSANCE

A Colette Iual.

Et quand je lui ai répondu 19
il m'a répondu 19
22 si tu as le temps d'être riche
30 et 40 pour la comédie en deux temps
50 pour ton sale anniversaire
100 pour les commodités du printemps
Pour le reste je suis pâle et hypnotique
mais occupez-vous de vos pavés cher docteur
et laissez à l'eau claire le soin de devenir de l'eau sale

MYSTERY OF MY BIRTH

To Colette Iual

And when I answered him 19
he answered me 19
22 if you have the time to be rich
30 and 40 for the comedy in two steps
50 for your nasty anniversary
100 for the commodities of spring
For the rest I am pale and hypnotic
but busy yourself with your lozenges dear doctor
and leave to fresh water the worry of becoming dirty water

LE MEILLEUR ET LE PIRE

Un enfant sérieux par la force des choses
attendait la naissance d'un animal
son frère
en expliquant les miracles de la mer

Lorsque le soleil se leva
sur une montagne de verveine
qui était une femme désirable
il se fit à travers la campagne
un grand bruit de vaisselle brisée
qui présageait l'approche d'un fléau

Une montagne de verveine

La montagne n'attendait qu'un souffle
venu de l'océan Pacifique
comme l'écho d'un désastre
pour remplacer le soleil
Et l'enfant cessa d'expliquer pour prédire

Alors se révéla chez les cruels les sanguinaires et les inassouvis
un grand désir de vins et de poison
Les uns partirent à la recherche de la fleur
qui n'éclôt qu'à la bonne époque chez les femmes parfaites
les autres voulaient faire un caillou
avec du sang et des larmes

Les uns et les autres disparurent dans l'océan Pacifique
près d'une île de phosphore
pour avoir confondu
les femmes spirituelles avec le souvenir du temps
et les plaisirs des sauvages

THE BEST AND WORST

A serious child by necessity
waited for the birth of an animal
his brother
while explaining the miracles of the sea

When the sun rose
on a mountain of vervain
which was a desirable woman
one could hear across the countryside
a loud noise of broken crockery
which prefigured the approach of a plague

A mountain of vervain

The mountain waited only for a breeze
coming from the Pacific Ocean
like the echo of a disaster
in order to replace the sun
And the child stopped explaining to predict

Then among the cruel the bloodthirsty and the insatiable
a great desire for wine and fish revealed itself
Some of them left in search of the flower
which bloomed only at the golden era among perfect women
the others wanted to make a stone
with blood and tears

One bunch and the others disappeared in the Pacific Ocean
near an island of phosphorus
from having confused
spiritual women with the memory of time
and the pleasures of savages

LES OSSEMENTS S'AGITENT

Lorsque du cerveau jaillit la palme sombre
l'oiseau mangeur de bananes
la lumière qui tombe comme des paupières de sommeil
le cheval et son cavalier s'agitent séparément
et crient j'ai faim
Une langue de sang passe le long de leurs nerfs
de leurs yeux coulent les poisons aimés du genre humain
les poisons que les femmes iront chercher sur les montagnes
les frissons qui passent avec la rapidité de l'éclair
sur ceux qui seront malades
les frissons de la rue qui sent le chien

Lorsque du cerveau jaillit la palme sombre
La main se pose sur la plante ou sur l'homme qui n'a qu'une dent
et la voix incolore sort du rocher de feu
Elle ordonne
Maintenant tu vivras sur la mer
comme les fumées des peuples assemblés

La lumière tombe comme des paupières de sommeil
et dix millions d'oiseaux au plumage ensanglanté
s'abattent sur l'arc de triomphe.

THE BONES RATTLE

When from the brain surges the dark palm tree
the bird eater-of-bananas
light that falls like eyelids of sleep
the horse and its rider move separately
and cry I'm hungry
A tongue of blood passes along their nerves
from their eyes flow poisons beloved of the human kind
poisons that the women will go to find on the mountains
shivers that pass with the quickness of lightning
shivers of the street that the dog senses

When from the brain surges the dark palm tree
The hand settles on the plant or on the man who has only one tooth
and the clear voice comes from the rock of fire
It commands
Now you will live on the sea
like the smoke of the assembled peoples

Light falls like eyelids of sleep
and ten million birds with bloodied plumage
beat down on the arc de triomphe

L'ARDEUR DÉSESPÉRÉE

Si le vent le permet
le désespoir ravagera les contrées saines
voisines de l'arc-en-ciel et du pôle de soie
la contrée où les visions des hyménoptères se concrétisent
où l'espoir des uns anime l'ardeur sexuelle des autres
où je passe comme une douleur périodique
qui stimule l'énergie des insectes à carapace de verre

O soupirs insectes d'avenir
je vous attends dans l'ombre que vous connaissez
pour vous confier des secrets qui vous donneront à réfléchir
des secrets si fluides qu'ils couleront entre vos doigts
comme les minutes entre les cuisses d'une jolie femme
et le sommeil des insensés
au soleil
à midi

DESPERATE ARDOR

If the wind allows it
despair will ravage healthy lands
neighbors of the rainbow and of the silk pole
land where visions of the hymenoptera come true
where the hope of some sparks the sexual ardor of others
where I pass by like a recurring sorrow
which stimulates the energy of glass-shelled insects

Oh sighs insects of the future
I wait for you in the shadow that you know
to confide in you secrets that will make you reflect
secrets so fluid they will run between your fingers
like minutes between the thighs of a pretty woman
and the sleep of the insane
in the sun
at noon

CŒUR DÉCROCHÉ

Danser sur le neuf de cœur
lever le pied de l'échafaud
passer et repasser le long des colonnes montantes
voiler d'un crêpe la terrine de foie gras
découvrir une racine dans sa tasse de café
élever trois mouches dans l'abbaye de Westminster
envoyer une carotte par la poste
dresser l'arbre généalogique d'un bec de gaz
s'égarer dans le tuyau de la pompe
voilà les plaisirs réservés au grain de poussière qui détraque les machines
    parfaites
les machines qui s'agitent comme des poissons

Les fusils aimantés de l'espèce des ombellifères
pendaient aux persiennes closes
leurs canons engagés dans les fentes
menaçaient les multiples serpents de l'ombre
ceux qui s'enroulent autour des bicyclettes
et ceux qui flottent le soir comme des mains tendues d'une rive à l'autre
Mais qu'une rive s'égare au cours de ce voyage
et tout est perdu comme dans une clache à plongeur

Le coup partit
Le rayon de soleil qui passait à travers un prisme ne se reconnut pas à la
    sortie
Il y eut un son de cloche étouffé
suivi du fruit sourd d'un paquet de linge qui tombe dans un puits
Et ce fut tout
Mais une roue remplaçait la main partie avec la rive

HEART HUNG UP

To dance on the nine of hearts
to raise the base of the scaffold
to pass and return along rising columns
veil with a crêpe the dish of foie gras
discover a root in one's cup of coffee
to raise three flies in Westminster Abbey
send a carrot by mail
to put up the family tree with a gas lamp
get lost in the hose pump
here are the pleasures reserved for a speck of dust which derails perfect
    machines
machines which wriggle like fish

Guns magnetized by a type of umbellifer
were hanging from the closed shutters
their barrels inserted in the slats
they menaced the multiple serpents of shadow
those that coil around bicycles
and those that float at night like hands extended from one shore to
    another
But if the shore strays in the course of this voyage
then all is lost as in a diving bell

The shot fired
The ray of sun that passed through a prism did not know itself at the
    exit
There was a muffled bell sound
followed by the muffled noise of a parcel of laundry that fell in a well
And that was all
But a wheel replaced the departed hand with the shore

J'IRAI VEUX TU

Il était une grande maison
sur laquelle nageait un scaphandrier de feu

Il était une grande maison
ceinte de képis et de casques dorés

Il était une grande maison
pleine de verre et de sang

Il était une grande maison
debout au milieu d'un marécage

Il était une grande maison
dont le maître était de paille
dont le maître était un hêtre
dont le maître était une lettre
dont le maître était un poil
dont le maître était rose
dont le maître était un soupir
dont le maître était virage
dont le maître était un vampire
dont le maître était une vache enragée
dont le maître était coup de pied
dont le maître était une voix caverneuse
dont le maître était une tornade
dont le maître était une barque chavirée
dont le maître était une fesse
dont le maître était la *Carmagnole*
dont le maître était la mort violente

Dites-moi dites-moi où est la grande maison

I'LL GO WANT TO

There was a big house
on which swam a deep-sea diver of fire

There was a big house
girded with kepis and gold helmets

There was a big house
full of glass and blood

There was a big house
standing in the middle of a swamp

There was a big house
whose master was made of straw
whose master was a beech
whose master was a letter
whose master was a hair
whose master was a rose
whose master was a sigh
whose master was a turn
whose master was a vampire
whose master was a mad cow
whose master was a kick
whose master was a deep voice
whose master was a tornado
whose master was a capsized boat
whose master was a butt cheek
whose master was the *Carmagnole**
whose master was violent death

Tell me tell me where's the big house

* This is a revolutionary song.

L'ENNEMI SECOUE SES PUCES

Personnage étranger
aux yeux d'écorce et d'amandes amères
tu es forcené sale pauvre et décadent
tu ouvres la bouche pour avaler tes chaussures
tu ouvres la bouche pour vomir le paysage
et le paysage te ressemble
Vous vous promenez bras dessus bras dessous
à la recherche d'une épingle de nourrice
celle qui a piqué un vieillard
dont la barbe métallique
l'habillait comme le meilleur tailleur
vous vous promenez de l'est à l'ouest
en croquant du sucre
pour apaiser vos sens qu'excite un soleil sexuel
A quoi est-ce que ça ressemble docteur
au tétanos ou à l'influenza
A un fromage ou à un merle
a un merle
le merle s'envole en sifflant
J'ai du bon papa dans ma papetière
J'ai du bon papa etc

Et tout le monde est content
sauf moi
car j'ai une sangsue sur l'œil

THE ENEMY BEATS HIM

Strange character
with eyes of bark and bitter almonds
you are frenzied dirty poor and decadent
you open your mouth to swallow your slippers
you open your mouth to vomit the landscape
and the landscape resembles you
You walk with arms around one another
looking for a safety pin
the one that pricked an old man
whose metallic beard
dressed him like the best tailor
you walk from east to west
crunching sugar
to appease your senses that a sexual sun excites
What does this resemble doctor
tetanus or flu
a cheese or a blackbird
a blackbird
the blackbird flies off whistling
I have some good papa in my paper maker
I have some good papa etc*

And everyone is happy
except me
because I have a leech on my eye

* These lines play on a popular French children's song, "J'ai du bon tabac dans ma
tabatière" ("I have some good tobacco in my snuff box").

L'ÉVOLUTION D'UNE JOLIE FEMME

C'était je m'en souviens un homme couleur de feu
Ses pieds dans un feu de paille
flambaient comme un soleil couchant
et ses mains inaltérables
étranglaient la dernière sœur de la dernière vierge
D'un arbre naît la femme
l'impénétrable aux yeux feuilles
qui lui demande de s'endormir
Il sait bien que s'il s'endort
il ne sera plus que flamme que dis-je fumée
et son étreinte se resserre
autour du cou qui brille comme un miroir
Le miroir voudrait être le cou
Il n'y a pas de désir qui tienne
Une goutte d'eau tombe sur ma tête
et j'en suis ébloui

THE EVOLUTION OF A PRETTY WOMAN

There was I recall a man color of fire
His feet in a fire of straw
were blazing like a sunset
and his steadfast hands
were strangling the last sister of the last virgin
From a tree woman is born
the impenetrable one with her leaf eyes
who asks him to sleep
He knows well that if he sleeps
he will be no more than flame what am I saying smoke
and his grip tightens
around the neck that shines like a mirror
The mirror would like to be the neck
There's no desire that lasts
A drop of water falls on my head
and by it I'm dazzled

LA VRAIE VIE

Un œil de daim
me promet une plaque de tôle
me donne un journal
et me coupe un bras

Je cours droit devant moi
autant que je puis m'en rendre compte
comme un poil de barbe emporté par le vent
Demain
je serai ce flocon de neige que tu envies
ce flocon de neige
qui deviendra grand
ce flocon de neige
qui ressemble à un chien
lors de la saison printanière

REAL LIFE

A deer's eye
promises me a sheet of metal
gives me a newspaper
and cuts off my arm

I run straight ahead
as far as I can tell
like a whisker carried by the wind
Tomorrow
I will be this snowflake that you envy
this snowflake
that will become big
this snowflake
that resembles a dog
during his spring season

LES ODEURS DE L'AMOUR

S'il est un plaisir
c'est bien celui de faire l'amour
le corps entouré de ficelles
les yeux clos par des lames de rasoir

Elle s'avance comme un lampion
Son regard la précède et prépare le terrain
Les mouches expirent comme un beau soir
Un banque fait faillite
entraînant une guerre d'ongles et de dents

Ses mains bouleversent l'omelette du ciel
foudroient le vol désespéré des chouettes
et descendent un dieu de son perchoir

Elle s'avance la bien-aimée aux seins de citron
Ses pieds s'égarent sur les toits
Quelle automobile folle
monte du fond de sa poitrine
Vire débouche et plonge
comme un monstre marin

C'est l'instant qu'ont choisi les végétaux
pour sortir de l'orbite du sol
Ils montent comme une acclamation
Les sens-tu les sens-tu
maintenant que la fraîcheur
dissout tes os et tes cheveux
Et ne sens-tu pas aussi que cette plante magique
donne à tes yeux un regard de main
sanglante
        épanouie

THE ODORS OF LOVE

If there's a pleasure
it's surely that of making love
the body surrounded by strings
eyes shut by razor blades

She glides like a paper lantern
Her glance precedes her and paves the way
Flies die like a beautiful evening
A bank fails
dragging a war of nails and teeth

Her hands upset the omelet of sky
strike with lightning the desperate flight of owls
and topple a god from his perch

She presses forward the beloved with lemony breasts
Her feet stray on roofs
What crazy automobile
rises from the depths of her chest
Veering it surges and plunges
like a sea monster

This is the moment vegetables have chosen
to leave earth's orbit
They rise like a cheer
Do you feel them do you feel them
now that coolness
dissolves your bones and your hair
And don't you also feel that this magical plant
makes your eyes look like a hand
bloody
       full blown

Je sais que le soleil
                    lointaine poussière
éclate comme un fruit mûr
si tes reins roulent et tanguent
dans la tempête que tu désires
Mais qu'importe à nos initiales confondues
le glissement souterrain des existences imperceptibles
il est midi

I know that the sun
                distant dust
bursts like a ripe fruit
if your loins roll and pitch
in the storm that you desire
But what does it matter to our merged initials
the underground sliding of imperceptible existences
it's noon

D'UNE VIE À L'AUTRE

Sur une roue tourne l'azur
O Azur qu'as-tu fait des cheveux blancs de la baronne
La baronne était une salve d'artillerie
qui crépitait à tout moment
pour empêcher les citoyens de dormir
Ceci pour le bonheur des citoyennes
Qui rendaient leur âme à une colonne de porphyre
en chantant
Hurrah Hurrah
Hurrah pour les chiens galeux
Hurrah pour les pavés de bois
Hurrah pour les femmes gelées
Hurrah pour le paradis dans la cave
Hurrah pour la Mésopotamie
Hurrah pour les éprouvettes
Hurrah pour les pendus
Hurrah pour les facteurs
Hurrah pour les automobiles
Hurrah pour les incendies
Hurrah pour les pelotes de laine
Hurrah pour les prisonniers
Hurrah pour les Arabes
Hurrah pour les satyres
et s'endormaient dans une feuille de fraisier
sans respirer
sans réfléchir aux conséquences de la chute d'une brique dans une mare
alors que le soleil
pied de zèbre
se pose sur les cheminées des Alpes
avec la légèreté d'une robe qu'on quitte
pour ne pas susciter de caprices chez les falaises bleues
qui se tordent
comme un serpent devant un puits de mine

FROM ONE LIFE TO THE OTHER

On a wheel turns the azure
Oh Azure what have you done with the white hair of the baroness
The baroness was a volley of artillery
that crackled at each moment
to keep citizens from sleeping
That's for the good of the citizens
Who gave their soul to a column of porphyry
singing
Hurrah Hurrah
Hurrrah for mangy dogs
Hurrah for tiles of wood
Hurrah for frozen women
Hurrah for paradise in a cave
Hurrah for Mesopotamia
Hurrah for test tubes
Hurrah for hanged men
Hurrah for mailmen
Hurrah for automobiles
Hurrah for fires
Hurrah for balls of wool
Hurrah for prisoners
Hurrah for the Arabs
Hurrah for the satyrs
and they were sleeping in a strawberry leaf
without breathing
without thinking of the consequences of a brick's fall into a pond
so that the sun
zebra foot
settles on the chimneys of the Alps
with the lightness of a dress that one slips off
in order not to stir caprices among the blue cliffs
which twist
like a snake in front of a mine shaft

UN OISEAU A FIENTÉ SUR MON VESTON SALAUD

A Pierre Naville.

Main vide et pied levé
le bon enfant sur deux assiettes
mourait d'envie de rire d'un cheval
solitaire
de la lune
de la rousse
Au lieu de mourir
il aurait pu rire
il préféra cogner comme un sourd
sur l'arbre le plus proche
L'arbre miaulait
T.S.F. T.S.F.
La T.S.F. le mordit au pied droit
et un ours à la main gauche
Comme il était jeune il n'en mourut pas
On le décora
on en fit un ambassadeur
Paul Claudel

A BIRD SHIT ON MY JACKET BASTARD

To Pierre Naville

Empty-handed and foot raised
the good child on two plates
was dying to laugh at a lonely
horse
at the moon
at the cops
Instead of dying
he could have laughed
he preferred to pound like a deaf man
on the nearest tree
The tree meowed
T.S.F. T.S.F.
The T.S.F.* bit him on the right foot
and a bear on the left hand
Since he was young he didn't die from it
They decorated him
made him an ambassador
Paul Claudel

* *Télégraphie sans fil.* Not in use any longer, refers to the radio telegraph.

CHARCUTONS *CHARCUTEZ*

A Suzanne Muzard.

Sur la carte il y a des lignes
qu'on appelle des golfes
Les enfants y mettent des grenouilles
qui leurs parents vont chercher
pour leur apprendre la vie
la civilisation
et leur faire connaître leurs devoirs envers la patrie

Inutile de dire que les grenouilles s'en foutent

Un jour où l'autre
un soldat
et une fermière
feront l'amour devant leurs poules
Elles en mourront
et sur leurs tombes naîtra un petit cul sec
qui saura danser le boston
ce sera la punition

Un soldat et une fermière

> Changement de viande rejouit le cochon

le cochon de chameau
le chameau de tramway
le tramway de papier

Si un bandit passait par là
vous verriez les yeux du soldat
se dilater comme un ballon captif

LET'S BUTCHER *GO BUTCHER*

To Suzanne Muzard

On the map there are lines
called gulfs
Children put frogs there
that their parents are going to look for
to teach them life
civilization
and to acquaint them with their patriotic duty

Useless to say that the frogs don't give a fuck

One day or the next
a soldier
and a farmwoman
will make love in front of their chickens
They will die of it
and on their tombs will be born a little bottoms up
which will know how to dance the boston
That will be the punishment

A soldier and a farmwoman

> Changing of meat gladdens the pig

the pig of a camel
the streetcar camel
the streetcar of paper

If a bandit passed by there
you would see the eyes of the soldier
dilate like a captive balloon

et les mains de la fermière
se couvrir de fermiers
Mais cela ne sera ne sera pas ne sera pas
et c'est dommage

and the hands of the farmwoman
get covered with farmers
But that will not be will not be will not be
and it's a pity

ILS ÉTAIENT DE CONNIVENCE

Que dit l'arc-en-ciel du vagin
au petit sauvage
habillé de vert-de-gris

Le vagin était nu
comme le sauvage

Il n'avait plus l'âge de mentir
moins encore de gémir
moins encore de chatouiller
le nombril du village voisin
Hé hé
Ce n'est pas prudent
pensait le village voisin
Sait-on jamais
si du nombril
les derniers couvercles
allaient jaillir comme un mâle
sans être précédés d'une lanterne
qu'est-ce qui ne rirait plus

THEY WERE COMPLICIT

What did the vagina's rainbow say
to the little savage
dressed in verdigris

The vagina was naked
like the savage

It was no longer young enough to lie
less still to moan
less still to tickle
the navel of the nearby village
Heh heh
It's not wise
thought the nearby village
Does one ever know
if from the navel
the last lids
were going to spurt like a bull
not being led by a lantern
what wouldn't laugh harder

UNE FEMME FATALE

Sur la Normandie qui pleure des larmes de cire
une feuille de thuya s'est posée
qui tremble à tous les vents des ports déserts
Elle est pauvre
elle est jaune
elle la sœur d'une dame aux yeux de sapinière
qui se tient à droite des pendus
la main sur le cœur
Un sourire large comme une goutte d'eau
flotte devant elle
et se perd dans la nuit

A FEMME FATALE

On Normandy which cries tears of wax
a thuja leaf has settled
that trembles with all the winds from deserted ports
It is poor
it is yellow
it is the sister of a lady with plantation eyes
who stands to the right of the hanged
hand on her heart
A big smile like a drop of water
floats before her
and gets lost in the night

LA DOUCEUR DU FOYER

La dame toussait toussait
le monsieur pâlissait
leur fils les doigts dans le nez
attendait l'apparition d'un bec de gaz sur sa poitrine
La dame toussait
depuis qu'elle avait vu
une femme blonde
fendre un rocher
avec un rasoir céleste
Si le monsieur pâlissait
c'était que le ciel le lui avait ordonné
en jonchant la terre de plumes de colibri
un colibri ainsi déplumé chanta
J'ai une queue
nom de Dieu
j'ai une queue
alors un grand souffle
fait de baleines de parapluies parfumées
passa sur la terre salée
comme la bénédiction d'une marchande de programmes
et trois colombes blanches
marquées d'une croix rouge
s'envolèrent du Mont-Blanc

DOMESTIC BLISS

The woman coughed coughed
the man grew pale
their son fingers in his nose
waited for the apparition of a gas lamp on his chest
The woman coughed
since she had seen
a blonde woman
split a rock
with a celestial razor
If the man grew pale
it was because heaven had ordered him to
strewing the earth with hummingbird feathers
a hummingbird thus plucked sang
I have a tail
God damn it
i have a tail
then a great breath
made of ribs of perfumed umbrellas
passed by on the salty earth
like the benediction of a seller of programs
and three white doves
marked with a red cross
flew off from Mont Blanc

LES MORTS ET LEURS ENFANTS

A Denise Kahn.

Si j'étais quelque chose
non quelqu'un
je dirais aux enfants d'Édouard
fournissez
et s'ils ne fournissaient pas
je m'en irais dans la jungle des rois mages
sans botes et sans caleçon
comme un ermite
st il y aurait sûrement un grand animal
sans dents
avec des plumes
et tondu comme un veau
qui viendrait une nuit dévorer mes oreilles
Alors dieu me dirait
tu es un saint parmi les saints
tiens voici une automobile
L'automobile serait sensationnelle
huit roues deux moteurs
et au milieu un bananier
qui masquerait Adam et Ève
faisant

mais ceci fera l'objet d'un autre poème

THE DEAD AND THEIR CHILDREN

To Denise Kahn

If I was something
not someone
i would say to Edward's children
provide
and if they did not provide
i would go off into the jungle of the three kings
without boots and without shorts
like a hermit
and surely there would be a big animal
without teeth
with feathers
and sheared like a calf
which would come one night to devour my ears
Then god would say to me
you are a saint among saints
look here's an automobile
The automobile would be sensational
eight wheels two engines
and in the middle a banana tree
that would conceal Adam and Eve
doing

but that will be the object of another poem

EN DEUX TEMPS ET TROIS MOUVEMENTS

Le vieux chameau désorganisé
dit à la demoiselle des P.T.T.
Une petite chaise s. v. p.
La demoiselle voulait une étoile
L'étoile voulait des bas de soie
Alors la demoiselle
le poing à la hauteur de toutes les circonstances
découvrit les cactus et les aima
Ce n'était pas sérieux
car les cactus aiment les alcools
et se rient des demoiselles
qui veulent des étoiles

IN DOUBLE TIME AND THREE MOVEMENTS

The old disorganized camel
said to the young lady of the Post. Tel & Tel.*
A little chair if y. pl.
The young lady wanted a star
The star wanted silk stockings
So the young woman
her fist rising to every occasion
discovered cacti and loved them
That was not serious
because the cacti love liqueurs
and don't give a damn about young ladies
who want stars

* The equivalent of UPS.

LA CHAIR HUMAINE

Une femme charmante qui pleurait
habillé de noir et de gris
m'a jeté par la fenêtre du ciel
Ah que la chute était grande ce jour où mourut le cuivre
Longtemps la tête pleine de becs d'oiseaux multiformes
j'errai alentour des suaires
et j'attendai devant les gares
qu'arrive le corbillard qui en fait sept fois le tour
Parfois une femme au regard courbe
m'offrait son sein ferme comme une pomme
Alors j'étais pendant des jours et des jours
sans revoir la nuit et ses poissons
Alors j'allais par les champs bordés de jambes de femme
cueillir la neige et les liquides odorants
dont j'oignais mes oreilles
afin de percevoir le bruit que font les mésanges en mourant
Parfois aussi une vague de feuilles et de fruits
déferlait sur mon échine
me faisait soupirer
après l'indispensable vinaigre
Et je courais et je courais à la recherche de la pierre folle
que garde une jambe céleste
Un jour pourtant plein d'une brumeuse passion
je longeais un arbre abattu par le parfum d'une femme rousse
Mes yeux me précédaient dans cet océan tordu
comme le fer par la flamme
et écartaient les sabres emmêlés
J'aurais pu forcer la porte
enroulée autour d'un nuage voluptueux
mais lassé des Parques et autres Pénélopes
je courbai mon front couvert de mousses sanglantes
et cachai mes mains sous le silence d'une allée
Alors vint une femme charmante

HUMAN FLESH

A charming woman who was crying
dressed in black and grey
threw me out the window of the sky
Ah what a long fall that day when copper died
Long my head full of beaks of multiform birds
I wandered around the shrouds
and I waited in front of the stations
for the hearse to arrive that circles them seven times
Sometimes a woman with a crooked glance
offered me her breast firm as an apple
Then I existed for days and days
without seeing night and its fish again
Then I went through fields bordered with women's legs
to gather snow and fragrant liquids
with which I anointed my ears
in order to perceive the noise that titmice make when dying
Sometimes also a wave of fruit and leaves
unfurled on my spine
making me sigh
for indispensable vinegar
And I ran and I ran in search of the mad stone
that a heavenly leg guards
One day however full of a misty passion
I walked along a tree felled by a redhead's perfume
My eyes preceded me in this ocean twisted
like iron by flame
and they parted tangled sabers
I could have forced the door
wrapped around a voluptuous cloud
But weary of the Fates and the other Penelopes
I bent my brow covered with bloody froth
and hid my hands beneath the silence in an alley
Then a charming woman arrived

habillée de noir et de gris
qui me dit
Pour l'amour des meurtres
tais-toi
Et emporté par le courant
j'ai traversé des contrées sans lumière et sans voix
où je tombais sans le secours de la pesanteur
où la vie était l'illusion de la croissance
jusqu'au jour éclairé par un soleil de nacre
où je m'assis sur un banc de sel
attendant le coup de poignard définitif

dressed in black and grey
who said to me
For the love of murders
shut up
And carried away by the current
I crossed countries without light and voiceless
where I fell without the help of gravity
where life was the illusion of growth
until the day lit up by a pearly sun
when I sat on a bench of salt
waiting for the dagger's final thrust

$$x = \infty \times \pi$$

La crue du fleuve prédispose ses rives obscures
aux plus obscurs désirs
La faim avec ses lèvres de volcan
viendra ensuite dans un rayon de soleil
arc-en-ciel de l'espoir et de l'erreur
demander des comptes au plus humble citoyen du pays

Que lui répondra-t-il
si ce n'est que la matière est plastique comme un calorifère
que la vie est le miel des animaux malfaisants
que les massacres continueront tant que durera la vie
tant que les enfants mort-nés se trouveront sur le passage d'Apollon

$$x = \infty \times \pi$$

The rise of the river predisposes its obscure banks
to the most obscure desires
Hunger with its volcano lips
will come next in a ray of sun
rainbow of hope and of error
to hold responsible the most humble citizens of the land

How will he respond to it
if not that matter is plastic like a heat pipe
that life is the honey of wicked animals
that massacres will continue as long as life goes on
as long as stillborn children find themselves on the Apollonian way

LE SANG RÉPANDU

La cendre qui est la maladie du cigare
imite les concierges descendant l'escalier
alors que leur balai tombé du quatrième étage a tué l'employé du gaz
cet employé semblable a un insecte sur une salade
L'oiseau guette l'insecte et le balai t'a tué employé
Ta femme aura des cheveux blancs comme le sucre
et ses oreilles seront des traites impayées
impayées parce que tu es mort
Mais cet employé que n'avait-il les pieds en forme de 3
que n'avait-il le regard lucide d'un magasin de gants
que n'avait-il pendant sur l'abdomen le sein desséché de sa mère
que n'avait-il des mouches dans les poches de son veston
Il eût passé humide et froid comme une potiche brisée
et ses mains eussent caressé les verrous de sa prison
Mais le soleil de sa poche avait mis sa casquette

SPILLED BLOOD

Ash which is the sickness of the cigar
imitates concierges coming down the stairs
after their broom fallen from the fourth floor killed the gas man
this worker resembling an insect on a salad
The bird watches for the insect and the broom killed you worker
Your wife's hair will be white as sugar
and her ears will be unpaid bills
unpaid because you're dead
But this worker why didn't he have feet in the shape of 3
why didn't he have the clear look of a glove store
why didn't he have hanging from his belly the dried breast of his
    mother
why didn't he have flies in his vest pockets
He would have died damp and cold like a broken vase
and his hands would have caressed the bars of his prison
But the sun in his pocket had put on its helmet

QU'IMPORTE

Que l'eau s'écoule comme un lampion
et je la rattraperai une nuit devant la mairie
à l'instant où une étoile filante
la seule de cette nuit-là
m'apprendra qu'une catastrophe a eu lieu au kilomètre 1000
Dans le train il y aura un sauvage
un vrai avec des moustaches de fumée emportée par le vent
Il y aura aussi une amazone
et tous deux se retrouveront côte à côte sur le ballast
Ils se féliciteront l'un et l'autre d'être sains et saufs
et se regarderont comme on regarde une forteresse en ruines s'écrouler
    du haut d'une colline
dans la vallée
en renversant un grand nombre de voitures chargées d'oranges
L'année prochaine la fleur d'oranger sera pour rien
et il y aura aussi beaucoup de malades
Jusqu'aux arbres qui seront épileptiques
et secoueront leur écorce sur les fiancés

Un petit bateau passe au fil de l'eau
mais ce n'est pas une étoile filante
il est trainé par un noyé
dont les longues dents effraient les poissons qui jaillissent comme des
    baïonnettes
se jettent dans des poitrines transparentes
et repartent vers d'autres poitrines
Mais le noyé sort de l'eau et flotte comme un drapeau rouge
Il claque des mains et des dents
son testament est dans une bouteille qui sort de sa bouche
comme un oiseau de son œuf
En souvenir de leur rencontre le sauvage et l'amazone se marieront

WHAT DOES IT MATTER

Let water slip by like a paper lantern
and I will catch it one night in front of town hall
at the instant when a shooting star
the only one of that particular night
will teach me that a catastrophe took place at kilometer 1000
In the train there will be a wild man
a real one with moustaches of smoke carried off by the wind
There will also be an Amazon
and the two of them will find themselves side by side on the ballast
They will congratulate each other on being safe and sound
and will look at each other the way one looks at a fortress in ruins
    crumbling from the top of a hill into the valley
overturning a great number of cars loaded with oranges
The next year the orange tree flower will be for naught
and there will also be many sick people
Extending to the trees which will be epileptic
and will shake their bark on the fiancés

A little boat goes by on the stream of water
but it is not a shooting star
it is dragged by a drowned man
whose long teeth scare the fish which shoot out like bayonets
hurl themselves into transparent chests
and leave again toward other chests
But the drowned man leaves the water and floats like a red flag
He claps his hands and teeth
His will is in a bottle that emerges from his mouth
like a bird from its egg
In memory of their meeting the wild man and the amazon will marry

dans la mairie d'un petit village inondé
et ce sera la barque traînée par le noyé qui les conduira au maire
lequel leur fera le speech d'usage en mangeant du cirage

at the town hall of a little flooded village
and it will be the boat dragged by the drowned man that will lead them
   to the mayor
who will give them the customary speech while eating shoe polish

LE GENOU FENDU

L'épaule indifférente
et la bouche malade
sont tombées sur les épines
comme les roses
Un œil les regarde
et s'envolera bientôt
à moins qu'une lumière
ne sorte de l'eau
avec une carpe
pour que tous les poils s'envolent vers le pôle

SPLIT KNEE

The indifferent shoulder
and the sick mouth
have fallen on thorns
like roses
An eye looks at them
and will fly off soon
unless a light
comes out of the water
with a carp
so that all the hairs fly off toward the pole

LE PIRATE ME DÉVORE

Maintenant que le bouchon s'est envolé vers d'autres cieux
il faut se couper les pieds
et les offrir en hommage à la première tomate mûre
A vrai dire c'est un hommage
ou une injure
L'avenir décidera
Aujourd'hui je suis assis sur un arbre millénaire
qui me donne d'excellents conseils
parce qu'il est millénaire
Une vieille femme me demande l'aumône
et je lui donne une cervelle de chevreuil
en lui disant
Dieu vous rendra un sabot
Je ne suis pas jeune non plus
mais je ne suis pas millénaire
c'est là mon tort
si j'étais millénaire j'entendrais les soupirs des écorces mûres
des savates de plomb et des derniers coups de fusil
qui tueront les derniers esclaves des derniers animaux insensibles

THE PIRATE DEVOURS ME

Now that the cork has flown toward other skies
we must cut off our feet
and offer them in tribute to the first ripe tomato
To tell the truth it's a tribute
or an insult
The future will decide
Today I am sitting on a thousand-year-old tree
that gives me excellent advice
Because it is a thousand years old
An old lady asks me for alms
and I give her a deer's brain
while telling her
God will give you a hoof
I am not young any more
but I am not a thousand years old
that's my flaw
if I were a thousand years old I would hear the sighs of ripe barks
of the slippers of lead and of the last gunshots
which will kill the last slaves of the last cold-hearted animals

SANS PRÉCÉDENT

Longues moustaches et larmes d'hydrogène
voilà l'animal féroce qui désole les mécaniques
Aujourd'hui
il se tord auprès d'une demoiselle et d'un violon
Le violon sent la rue et les poissons
et s'éloigne de la demoiselle
comme la balle du fusil
Et l'animal se tord toujours
et le violon arrive à Toronto
Il défonce un gratte-ciel rempli de colibris
qui s'envolent jusqu'à Panama
où il bouchent le canal
Et la demoiselle seule et triste
coupe des oranges pour une vieille sorcière
qui a planté des dés à coudre
dans une coupe à champagne
les dés ont fleuri
Ils abritent une légion de moustiques
qui se croient aux ballets russes
quoique la saison soit terminée
et dansent une danse mystique
à l'ombre d'un parapluie
Oh mademoiselle vous pleurez des larmes de caoutchouc
qui blessent votre concierge
Votre concierge s'ennuie dans sa loge de cire
Elle attend un pneumatique
envoyé par le grand bananier du pape
Il fait le tour de l'Afrique
pour chasser les canards sauvages
Hélas hélas il n'a rencontré qu'un scorpion électrique et sacré
qui vivait dans une mandoline
Maintenant sur les rives glacées des lacs de serpents
il pêche mélancolique et muet

WITHOUT PRECEDENT

Long moustaches and tears of hydrogen
there's the ferocious animal that depresses mechanics
Today
it twists itself near a young lady and a violin
The violin smells the street and the fish
and moves away from the young lady
like a pistol shot
And the animal twists continually
and the violin arrives in Toronto
It smashes a skyscraper filled with hummingbirds
which fly to Panama
where they plug the canal
And the lady sad and alone
cuts oranges for an old sorcerer
who has planted thimbles
in a flute of champagne
the dice have flowered
They shelter a legion of mosquitoes
which believe they are at the ballet russe
although the season is over
and they dance a mystical dance
in the shadow of an umbrella
Oh mademoiselle you cry rubber tears
that wound your concierge
Your concierge is bored in her lodging of wax
She waits for a telegram
sent by the great banana tree of the pope
He's touring Africa
to hunt wild ducks
Alas alas he only met an electric and sacred scorpion
who was living in a mandolin
Now on the frozen banks of the lakes of serpents
he fishes melancholy and silent

un citron qui ne le consolera jamais
d'avoir perdu un jour acide
plein de jambes de femme de poils obscènes
une ombre sans douleur
qui tournait autour d'un arbre sans vertu

for a lemon which will never console him
for having lost an acid day
full of women's legs of obscene hairs
a shadow without sorrow
which turned around a tree without virtue

COU TORDU

A Michel Leiris.

Qu'il s'élance le ruisseau solidifié par les grandes branches du vent
qu'il s'élance du haut de la cathédrale de hannetons
qu'il s'élance sans crainte
car la crainte est attelée au buffet vermoulu des chaleurs moites
et son appel ressuscitera la grande muraille des têtes coupées
et la poussière la poussière aux ailes tordues par ses courantes intérieurs
n'hésitera pas à s'envoler
pour courir la chance d'un internement dans les racines de l'armée
quitte à s'évader à l'instant où les hommes
fatigués par leurs méditations sur les spasmes de l'horizon
tombent avec le bruit d'un nuage heurtant les poissons de ses rêves
et lui offrent l'alcôve de leurs floraisons intenses
Qu'ils s'étonne donc ce ruisseau aux écailles de cuivre
et que son élan le porte à l'orée de cette forêt liquide
dont les yeux étincelants regardent
et me répètent sans arrêt
La fumée s'échappe de ton cœur
et ce n'est pas celle d'une maison blanche dont les volets sont clos à
    cause de la nuit
Découvre le père de la fumée
et ton rire secouera les vertigineuses cohortes des rails perdus par les
    fantômes

TWISTED NECK

To Michel Leiris

Let the stream surge solidified by great branches of wind
let it surge from the height of the cathedral of June bugs
let it surge without fear
because fear is yoked to the worm-eaten buffet of muggy heat waves
and its call will resuscitate the great wall of chopped-off heads
and the dust the dust with wings twisted by its interior currents
will not hesitate to fly off
in order to run the risk of a burial in the roots of the army
why not escape at the instant when men
fatigued by their meditations on spasms of the horizon
are falling with the noise of a cloud hitting the fish of its dreams
and they offer it the alcove of their intense flowerings
Let this stream astonish then with scales of copper
and let its surge carries it to the edge of this liquid forest
whose sparkling eyes look at me
and constantly repeat me
The smoke escapes from your heart
and it is not that of a white house whose shutters are closed because
    of night
Discover the father of smoke
and your laughter will shake the dizzying cohorts of tracks lost by
    phantoms

LA BOÎTE AUX LUMIÈRES

Elle est pleine d'un coton léger
qui s'envole au moindre bruit
qui crépite au moindre vent
qui s'ennuie à la moindre pluie
et qui tue pour le moindre désir

Cela ne peut pas continuer ainsi
Il tombe sur les pieds de mon voisin
une mousse de nuages
qui est verte
Ce sont des épinards

Il tombe sur la tête de ma voisine
des cailloux de fourrure
dont elle fait ses délices
Ce sont des souris

THE BOX OF LIGHTS

It's full of a light cotton
that takes flight at the least noise
that crackles at the least breeze
that gets bored by the least rain
and that kills for the least desire

Things can't go on this way
There's falling on my neighbor's feet
a moss of clouds
that's green
It's spinach

Falling on my neighbor's head
pebbles of fur
in which she delights
They're mice

PLEIN LES BOTTES

L'oreille des lampes écoute les feuilles tomber dans le sel
Le sel aujourd'hui a la forme de son sein
et danse danse
Il dansera tout le jour et la nuit ne l'arrêtera pas
il dansera toute la nuit et le réveil des pierres ne l'arrêtera pas
il dansera ainsi jusqu'à ce que les chevaux de frise meurent
comme meurent les glaciers et les neiges
Pourtant lorsque la nuit me regardera doucement comme un cœur
les chevaux de frise sentiront leurs os se gonfler
les voiles les emporter sur des routes douteuses
où se traînent les cerveaux des reptiles sacrés
L'un d'eux dont la main s'allonge vers le portemanteaux du charbon
sourira au passage des chevaux de frise
Et cependant il passeront
Ils passeront si longtemps que leur souvenir se perdra
comme un chien dans la mer
comme un doigt dans un gant
comme une oreille dans un coquillage
etc et mille fois etc
car etc c'est la nuit des borgnes qui s'allonge comme un caoutchouc
et revient les frapper au visage
Il est vrai que leur visage est mort puisqu'ils sont borgnes
et que pour eux la nuit est morte puisqu'elle s'allonge
Mais le jour aux doigts de tulipe
le jour dont les soupirs disparaissent dans les caves de l'araignée
le jour enfin dont les regards tombent comme des fruits
le jour pour eux n'est plus qu'un petit bateau d'enfant
isolé dans une baignoire
et ils auront beau faire jamais la baignoire n'aura les oreilles d'un veau
jamais la baignoire ne cassera de noix à midi
jamais la baignoire ne tuera un chat
jamais la baignoire ne fera de veuves

FED UP

The ear of the lamps hears leaves falling in salt
Salt today has the form of her breast
and dances dances
It will dance all day and the night will not stop it
it will dance all night and the waking of stones will not stop it
it will dance like that until the Frisian horses die
as snows and glaciers die
However when night will look at me tenderly like a heart
the Frisian horses will feel their bones swell
the sails will carry them on dubious routes
where the brains of sacred reptiles crawl
One among them whose hand plunges toward the suitcase of coal
will smile at the passage of the Frisian horses
And nevertheless they will pass by
They will pass by for so long that their memory will disappear
like a dog in the sea
like a finger in a glove
like an ear in a shell
etc and thousand times etc
because etc it's the night the of one-eyeds that stretches like a rubber
    band
and snaps back to hit them in the face
It's true that their face is dead since they are one-eyed
and that for them the night is dead since it stretches out
But day with fingers of tulip
day whose sighs disappear in the spider's caves
day finally whose glances fall like fruits
day for them is no more than a child's toy boat
lonely in a bathtub
and whatever they do the bathtub will never have the ears of a calf
never will the bathtub crack a walnut at noon
never will the bathtub kill a cat
never will the bathtub make widows

car la baignoire est morte
la baignoire est morte comme le pain qui n'a jamais vécu
le pain qui est condamné à mort avant d'être pain
comme l'eau est condamnée à mort avant d'être eau

because the bathtub is dead
the tub is dead like the bread that never lived
bread that is condemned to death before being bread
as water is condemned to death before being water

L'ARÊTE DES SONS

Rien qu'un cri d'arbre mort
suffit pour l'insensible bonheur
Rien qu'un soleil de plâtre
sur les routes de flamme
me donne le vertige
et je suis semblable aux insectes sonores
qui couvrent les membres des martyrs
et leur valent une toison d'or
qui n'est désirée que par les athlètes invisibles des mines blanches
Si je leur ressemble c'est que la vie est pleine de coquilles
de soupapes d'échappement
et de virages sur des plaques de verre
tournant à l'inverse de la terre
La terre à ces moments-là s'allonge
dans son ennui
et tremble comme une feuille morte
La chaleur disparaît dans les manteaux des pèlerins
et la pluie s'éloigne
à la suite des navigateurs aux oreilles de bronze
Un grande roue tourne dans un vide bleu
et trois éléphants pêchent des requins
Une femme les yeux loin de la terre
et de ses falaises nacrées
s'élève lentement
rose épanouie

THE RIDGE OF SOUNDS

Nothing but a cry from a dead tree
suffices for numb happiness
Nothing but a plaster sun
on the roads of flame
gives me vertigo
and I am the same as sonorous insects
which cover the limbs of martyrs
and earn them a fleece of gold
which is desired only by invisible athletes with wan expressions
If I resemble them it's because life is full of shells
of escape valves
and of turns on the plates of glass
turning the opposite way from earth
The earth in those moments stretches
in its boredom
and trembles like a dead leaf
Warmth disappears in the cloaks of pilgrims
and the rain withdraws
following navigators with ears of bronze
A great wheel turns in a blue void
and three elephants fish for sharks
A woman her eyes far from the earth
and from its pearly cliffs
rises now
fullblown rose

UNE ÎLE DANS UNE TASSE

Les siècles de charbon les lanternes de colle sèche
les pertes de temps les chutes d'eau
se succèdent et se perdent dans l'allée grise qui mène aux îles sanglantes
Il n'y a pas plus de temps que d'eau
pas plus d'eau que d'éponges
et les feuilles tombent au fond des têtes obscures
Parfois un oiseau passe comme une main gelée
et comprime lourdement les gorges haletants
les gorges qui frémissent aussi parce que les méduses hantent les
    corridors
en hurlant si lugubrement que les raz de marée ne se retiennent plus
    de joie
et le cri qui s'en échappe alors
brûle les opéras et les cimetières
déchire le voile des mariées
qui n'ont plus aucune gêne à se montrer nues puisqu'elles sont mariées
et rend aphones les bêtes multicolores
qui vivent et se multiplient
dans le vin blanc
C'est le signal tant attendu par les frères du corail
qui cuvent leur ivresse dans les gares
où les chiens enragés concentrent leur colère
Lorsqu'ils reconnaîtront les mœllons qui les entourent
les mœllons enragés
ils se lèveront comme cette feuille de papier
qui craint le feu comme son ombre
et se jetteront l'un à l'autre
les os qui nuisent à leur légèreté
puis comme le soupirail sera trop étroit pour leur immense orgueil
ils s'enfonceront dans la terre comme des projectiles délirants

250

AN ISLAND IN A CUP

The centuries of coal the lanterns of dry glue
the wastes of time the waterfalls
follow each other and get lost in the grey alley that leads to the bleeding
    islands
There's no more weather than water
no more water than sponges
and leaves fall to the bottom of dark heads
Sometimes a bird passes by like a frozen hand
and tightly constricts gasping throats
gorges that quiver also because jellyfish haunt the corridors
howling so lugubriously that the tidal waves no longer hold joy
and the cry that escapes from them then
burns operas and cemeteries
tears the veil from brides
who have no longer have any qualm showing themselves naked since
    they are married
and render voiceless the multicolored beasts
that live and multiply
in white wine
It's the signal so long awaited by the brothers of coral
who sleep off their drunkenness in the stations
where rabid dogs focus their anger
When they will meet the cinderblocks that surround them
the furious cinderblocks
they will rise up like this sheet of paper
which fears fire like its shadow
and throw themselves at one another
the bones which detract from their lightness
then like the cellar window will be too narrow for their immense pride
they will sink deep in the earth like delirious projectiles

N'ATTENDEZ JAMAIS

Misère Le cheval sent reverdir le bois de ses veines
et son cavalier tache l'horizon comme un drapeau
Il est minuit et les chats dévident des pelotes de laine sur un cadavre
pendant que les vaches meuglent après le chef de gare
Il est minuit et le chef de gare maigrit dans son cahot
Il lèche le mure pour s'évader
et délivre les graffiti de leur prison

C'est un naufrage
La jeune fille étreint la queue d'un requin au lieu du cou de son fiancé
C'est un tremblement de terre
et l'Opéra est projeté dans le marché de la Villette
C'est l'exécution de Louis XVI
et la tête du supplicie rebondit sur celle de son épouse
qui s'évanouit

Lèche le mur chef de gare
Lèche le mur sans t'évader

NEVER WAIT

Woe The horse feels the wood of its veins grow green again
and its horseman stains the horizon like a flag
It's midnight and cats unwind balls of wool on a corpse
meanwhile cows moo after the stationmaster
It's midnight and the stationmaster grows thin in his dungeon
He licks the wall to escape
and frees the graffiti from its prison

It's a shipwreck
The young girl embraces the tail of a shark instead of the neck of her
    fiancé
It's an earthquake
and the Opera is thrown into the market of Villette
It's the execution of Louis XVI
and the head of the executed bounces on that of his wife
who faints

Lick the wall stationmaster
Lick the wall without escaping

LA LUMIÈRE DANS LE SOLEIL

La petite nudité
s'ennuie dans son mil bateau roux
Elle s'allonge comme la mer
comme ses cheveux
Elle demande à la pluie et au beau temps
une ramure de scies
et une corde d'évangile
avec de grandes chandelles de maisons
Elle est si jeunesse et si beauté
que la suie grande coquine
s'approche d'elle avec ses mains de cygne
nettoyées par l'alcool et les vents
Mais la pluie sourit au beau temps
qui caresse les poils des montagnes
et tous deux s'entendent pour chasser les vallées
qui vivent de feuilles et de poussière
de pierres et de bâtons

THE LIGHT IN THE SUN

The little nudity
is bored in her red millet boat
She stretches like the sea
like her hair
She asks from rain and from good weather
a rower of saws
and a gospel rope
with great home candles
She is so youth and so beauty
that soot huge naughty
approaches her with swanlike hands
cleaned by alcohol and the winds
But rain smiles at the good weather
which caresses the fur of the mountains
and both agree to hunt the valleys
which live on leaves and dust
stones and sticks

CHIEN ET CHAT

Dans le sentier des mains gelées glissent les oriflammes
Ils sont gris bleu vert rouge et ont la forme de mon visage
car je les ai faits semblables à mon rire
qui éclate dans la mousse comme une pierre qui s'envole
Et les pierres s'envolent chaque jour comme les ouvriers s'en vont à leur
    travail
car ils s'envolent pour travailler
et leurs usines sont dans les nuages
et les nuages sont vieux comme les escaliers qui mènent aux oranges de
    laine
et que montent et descendent les albatros de ma tête
Albatros c'est grâce à vous que ma tête me coupe les pieds
et que mes pieds sont de pâle vierges
maigres comme un dieu
Albatros Albatros si ma tête n'était pas en vous
elle aurait au moins la forme de votre bec
et mes ongles seraient dans votre bec
car ce sont eux qui ont fait ma tête
comme la terre fait l'eau
et comme l'eau use les cordes des arcs mal tendus pour la circonstance
Et les arcs les arcs mon dieu se noient dans la plaine submergée
qu'on appelle *As-tu vu ces idiots*
La plaine est tellement submergée qu'elle n'est déjà plus plaine
mais main
Encore un peu et elle sera ventre
puis torse

Enfin je reconnaîtrai son visage semblable à une forêt

DOG AND CAT

In the path of frozen hands slide banners
They are grey blue green red and take the form of my face
because I made them identical to my laughter
which bursts in the moss like a stone that flies off
And stones fly off each day the way workers leave for work
because they fly off to their jobs
and their factories are in the clouds
and the clouds are old like stairs which lead to oranges of wool
and which the albatrosses of my head climb and descend
Albatross it's thanks to you that my head chops off my feet
and that my feet are pale virgins
thin like a god
Albatross albatross if my head were not in you
it would have at least the form of your beak
and my nails would be in your beak
because it's they who made my head
like earth makes water
and like water wears out the ropes of bows badly fitted for the
    circumstances
And the bows the bows my god are drowning in the submerged plain
called *Have you seen these idiots*
The plain is so submerged that it's already no longer plain
but hand
Awhile longer and it will be belly
then torso

Finally I will recognize its face identical to a forest

LE QUART D'UNE VIE

QUARTER OF A LIFE

LE QUART D'UNE VIE

I

A l'intérieur
le catalogue vendait des huîtres vivantes
qui pleuraient et qui chantaient
sur un air américain

II

Les feuilles qui sont tombées
ont emporté les deux taxis
Les taxis ont renversé les sémaphores
Les sémaphores tombés
le lait ne coulera plus
car les moustaches tombées
ne repousseront plus

III

Nous sommes plus heureux que la mousse
la mousse n'a pas de cheveux
et nous portons de cheveux
Pauvres chapeaux aux ailes couvertes de givre
la fumée des cigarettes vous excite
mais le pétrole
le pétrole sournois qui vide les ostensoirs
est plus léger à vos reins
que les chaînes d'aluminium

QUARTER OF A LIFE

I

Inside
the catalogue was selling live oysters
that cried and sang
an American tune

II

The leaves that fell
swept away two taxis
The taxis overturned the signals
The signals down
milk will flow no more
because fallen moustaches
will grow back no more

III

We are happier than moss
moss has no hair
and we wear hats
Poor hats with wings covered with frost
smoke of cigarettes excites you
but oil
the sly oil which empties the monstrances
is lighter on your kidneys
than aluminum chains

IV

Croupissez regards des sulamites
Il pleut Il neige
Sous le soleil qui nous déteste
les chiens mangent la merde
les ceinturons s'enrichissent des sabots des vieux chevaux
qui les oreilles percées
le ventre lumineux
vendent leurs chemises aux portes des églises
sans se soucier des cachalots et des zébus
Jolis mois d'aout c'est le mois des zébus
Les zébus ont trop bu
bu bu bu et boira
boira qui voudra
mais ce n'est pas moi qui le voudrai
C'est trop laid le cervelet
qui sans sourire court à la chapelle
téléphoner aux parfumeurs

V

C'est un jour saint un jour sacré
un jour sacré à l'hôtel
Vivent les atlas sous les bateaux

VI

Plutôt que périssent les cannibales
nous démolirons les pianos
nous interdirons les vendanges
nous arrêterons les marées

IV

Go rot glances of the Sulamites
It rains It snows
Under the sun that detests us
dogs eat shit
belts grow rich off the wooden shoes of old horses
who pierced ears
stomachs luminous
sell their shirts at the doors of churches
without worrying about the sperm whales and the zebus
Fine month of August it's the month of the zebu
The zebus drank too much
drank drank drank and will drink
whoever wants to will drink
but it's not me who'll want to
That's too ugly the cerebellum
who without smiling runs to the chapel
to telephone the perfumers

V

It is a holy day a sacred day
a sacred day at the hotel
Long live atlases under the boats

VI

Rather than let cannibals perish
we'll smash pianos
we'll forbid grape harvests
we'll stop the tides

VII

Couverture des étoiles
le vent roule des motocyclettes
Il ne croit pas à l'eau salée
et symbolise les aspirations des peuples
comme la guerre
comme les vêtements

VIII

La cavalerie n'est pas loin
et les oscillations non plus

IX

Vers le ciel de juillet
montent les fourrures ovipares
Le serrurier militaire
invente le contrepoint
nécessaire à la nourriture des abeilles

X

L'éléphant sans moteur
naquit sans scandale
Absalon-la-main-verte lui sourit
et rangea les lis de ses viscères
sur un poteau
sur un épingle
Guetté par le scorbut
il sera veuf un jour
où la couleur changera comme la chaleur

VII

Blanket of stars
wind runs the motorcycles
It does not believe in salt water
and symbolizes the people's aspirations
like war
like clothing

VIII

The cavalry is not far
neither are fluctuations

IX

Toward the July sky
climb the oviparous furs
The military locksmith
invents the counterpoint
necessary for feeding bees

X

The elephant without motor
Was born without scandal
Absolom-the-green-hand smiled at him
and arranged the lilies of his viscera
on a post
on a pin
Threatened by scurvy
he will be a widower one day
when color will change like the heat

XI

Noble cœur songe au collodion
qui les pieds dans ses cheveux
s'ennuie s'ennuie s'ennuie
comme un bouquet de lilas
dans une valise

XII

Miroirs des balcons
les balcons sur les citernes
évitent les avirons
invitent les kangourous
visitent les ailes des moulins
et meurent comme les zouaves
sans océan et sans chaussettes
Ainsi soit-il

XIII

Le visage roulé dans la farine
le tropique du Capricorne est dans ma main
qui tremble
qui s'amincit et s'allonge
qui roule
et s'en va très loin sous un arbre
comme un rat malade

XI

Noble heart dreams of the collodion
who its feet in its hair
is bored bored bored
like the bouquet of lilacs
in a suitcase

XII

Mirrors of balconies
balconies on the cisterns
avoid rowboats
invite kangaroos
visit the blades of windmills
and die like the zouaves
without ocean and without socks
So be it

XIII

Face tricked in flour
the Tropic of Capricorn is in my hand
which trembles
which slims and spreads out
which rolls
and departs very far under a tree
like a sick rat

XIV

Vins et cheminée
allons-nous-en
Nos pieds ont leurs épingles
et les veaux leur mystère
Sans ministre ni harpon
allons-nous-en

XV

Il est temps de vous marier
si vous craignez la pluie
vieux monastère sans ceinture
plaques grises
coton de malheur

XVI

Alors de la gouttière
un membre mal fermé
dont le nom mal brossé
dégoulinait sur un poisson
s'enflamma sans dégoût
Sa destinée fut courte comme une sueur
Ma sœur
as-tu vu ma pipe
Ma pipe est morte
et mon grand œil est sans saveur

XIV

Wines and hearth
let's get going
Our feet have their pins
and the calves their mystery
Without minister or harpoon
let's go

XV

Time to get married
if you fear the rain
old beltless monastery
grey blotches
wretched cotton

XVI

So from the gutter
a limb badly closed
whose badly brushed name
was trickling on a fish
blazed without disgust
Its destiny was short like a sweat
My sister
have you seen my pipe
My pipe is dead
and my great eye is flavorless

LA PÊCHE EN EAU
TROUBLE

FISHING IN
TROUBLED WATER

LA PÊCHE EN EAU TROUBLE

I

Aux gants les mains
Aux innocents les gants
Aux gants les mains pleines
Avec les petites fleurs de manganèse étoilé
les arètes pulmonaires
qui voyagent sous l'arc-en-ciel
de midi à midi

II

L'homme pâle comme une cloche
célèbre comme une tortue
sans effort
sans douleur ni lumière
alluma son orteil
et devint chaste

III

Oui mais vive le rouge
cria la sorcière car il défend
Et les jeunes filles enceintes demanderont des rossignols
Et les vieillards malades apprendront la physique

FISHING IN TROUBLED WATER

I

To the gloves hands
To the innocents gloves
To the gloves full hands
With little flowers of starry manganese
pulmonary fishbones
that travel beneath the rainbow
from noon to noon

II

The man pale like a bell
famous like a tortoise
without effort
without sorrow or light
lit his toe
and became chaste

III

Yes but long live red
cried the witch because it protects
And young pregnant girls will ask for nightingales
And old sick people will learn physics

IV

Avec les nerfs des dentelles
les Suédois nourrissent les serpents
qui font croître leur famille
Avec des cadavres de crème
Ils s'envolent volent volent volent volent volent

V

La main du mystère est dans ma poche
et le mystère dans un aérostat
tourne sur l'étoile de son ventre
ses cheveux sont des cadeaux de mariage
Un oignon autour de sa ceinture assure sa virginité
Pentagone de l'âme
Beurre

IV

With nerves some lace
the Swedes nourish serpents
who make their families grow
With corpses of cream
They fly away fly fly fly fly fly

V

The hand of mystery is in my pocket
and the mystery in a balloon
turns on the star of its stomach
Its hairs are wedding gifts
An onion around its belt assures its virginity
Pentagon of the soul
Butter

LE TRAVAIL ANORMAL

ABNORMAL WORK

LE TRAVAIL ANORMAL

I

Si vous trouvez une bête noire dans une grange
faites qu'elle s'avance vers vous
en reculant
et remplacez son œil droit
par un marron d'Inde
artistement sculpté
Les meilleurs pigeons du canton
accourront vers vous
et se nicheront sous votre parapluie

II

Caravane caravane
Il n'est pas de meilleure heure
pour se saouler
que l'heure du berger

III

Pas d'oreilles ni de serments
Surveillez-vous bien surveillez-vous bien
des bandes de peau
se détacheront de votre poitrine
et vous n'y verrez rien

ABNORMAL WORK

I

If you find a black beast in a barn
make it charge you
drawing back
and replace its right eye
with a horse chestnut
artistically sculptured
The best pigeons of the county
will run up toward you
and nestle under your umbrella

II

Caravan caravan
There is no better time
to get drunk
than the shepherd's hour

III

Neither ears nor oaths
Watch yourself well watch yourself well
bands of skin
will peel from your chest
and you won't see a thing

IV

Quatre espaces blancs nous regardent
quatre espaces plus blancs que des cheveux
mais riches
quatre espaces qui sont quatre infinis
L'infini du serpent qui est horizontal
et ceux qui tournent
ou sautent comme des carpes
ou plongent
comme une pierre dans un arbre

V

O femmes des pierres
vos maries sont partis
et coupent des glaces
vos sexes sont usés comme un miroir
et vos pieds les remplacent
Vos maris sont partis
Dans la main de leur meilleur ami
vit un scarabée
léger et lucide
C'est la vie
Mais si vous regardez les plantes merveilleuses
qui s'agitent dans les tiroir secrets
un secret amour pour le jeu
et les étoiles filantes
occupera tous vos instants

IV

Four white spaces are looking at us
four spaces whiter than hair
but rich
four spaces which are four infinities
The infinity of the serpent who is horizontal
and those who turn
or jump like carp
or plunge
like a stone into a tree

V

Oh women of the stones
your husbands have left
and cut the ice
your sexes are worn like a mirror
and your feet replace them
Your husbands have left
In the hand of their best friend
lives a scarab
light and lucid
That's life
But if you look at the marvelous plants
which tremble in secret drawers
a secret love for gambling
and shooting stars
will occupy all your moments

VI

Vos pierres sont tordues par un simoun nocturne
Les enfants de vos enfants
sans chemise
croquent des os de rat

Fermons les serrures
et gravissons la colline malade
pour voir dormir les illustres vignerons
Alors les rats retrouveront leurs os moins un
qui sera le sternum
Un beau rat vaut un pays d'amour
dit la chanson
mais les rats sans sternum
auront perdu leur beauté
C'est pourquoi les enfants
en allant à l'école
croquent toujours des os de rat

VII

Courez vite et songez peu
c'est votre droit
c'est votre bras

VI

Your stones are twisted by a nocturnal simoom
The children of your children
shirtless
crunch rats' bones

Let's latch the locks
and climb the sick hill
to see famous winemakers sleep
Then rats will find their bones minus one
that will be the sternum
A handsome rat is worth a country of love
the song goes
but the rats without sternum
will have lost their beauty
That's why children
going to school
always crunch rat's bones

VII

Run fast and dream little
that's your right
that's your arm

VIII

Un ministère tombe
grattons grattons les éléphants
Un éléphant gratté
c'est du beurre pour les vieux ans
Un cervelle s'envole
Il est plus facile de porter une bague
que de défendre son chien
Connue pour son ventre
la mère du beau temps
roule sur le sable
un langue sur chaque pied

IX

Sans tabac pas de métro
dit la princesse
en comptant jusqu'à dix
Les fourrures sont riches
comme un millionnaire

X

Nous découvrirons Tombouctou
en faisant du skating
et ce sera une grande joie
car nous voulons vivre
sur une mer d'olives

XI

Olives olives olives olives

VIII

A ministry falls
let's scratch scratch the elephants
A scratched elephant
that's butter for old age
A brain flies off
It is easier to wear a ring
than to defend one's dog
Known for her stomach
the mother of good weather
rolls on the sand
a tongue on each foot

IX

Without tobacco no metro
says the princess
counting to ten
The furs are rich
like a millionaire

X

We will discover Timbuktu
while skating
and it will be a great joy
because we want to live
on a sea of olives

XI

Olives olives olives olives

XII

Un athlète qui rit
un chameau qui danse
un homme qui tue sa fille
un rat qui s'allume
une vache qui s'habille
une baleine qui monte dans une baleinière
une dame qui renonce
une vague
un dieu en voiture
un faux tremblement de terre
un marécage éclairé par une lanterne sourde
un meuble ouvert
un affreux sourire
Si vous n'êtes pas satisfait
voyez un docteur
qui ne guérira pas vos maladies

XIII

Si vous avez froid
regardez-vous dans un miroir
une langue à la place du sexe
Ne regardez pas la lune
Ne tirez pas la langue
La lune est ronde
et votre langue est loin
Et surtout ne perdez pas vos yeux
dans un pays lointain

XII

An athlete who laughs
a camel who dances
a man who kills his daughter
a rat who lights up
a cow who gets dressed
a whale who climbs into a whaleboat
a woman who renounces
a wave
a god on board
a false earthquake
a swamp lit by a dull lantern
an open piece of furniture
a frightful smile
If you are not satisfied
see a doctor
who will not cure your ailments

XIII

If you're cold
look at yourself in a mirror
a tongue there in place of sex
Don't look at the moon
Don't stick out your tongue
The moon is round
and your tongue's far away
And above all don't lose your eyes
in a far-off country

XIV

Glandes salivaires et autres
Tombées sur le chapeau d'une jeune fille
vous perpétuerez
la race des hommes suaves
car il est écrit
Vite Agnès
Agnès grandit en force et en beauté
et sauva du néant
les oiseaux à corne blanche

XV

L'enfant du cerveau
n'aura pas les yeux bleus
Les yeux bleus sont trop verts
et peuvent tomber dans la mer
La mer de savon
qui roule des cigares neufs
destinés aux luxures guerrières
ne néglige point les yeux
Les yeux aiment le cuivre
et le cuivre est trop vert dans la mer
Alors les yeux sur l'aile d'un albatros
quitteront les mers pâles
pour les salons fermés
et rouleront à jamais
sur les pianos maudits

XIV

Salivary glands and others
Fallen on the hat of a young girl
you perpetuate
the race of suave men
because it's written
Quickly Agnes
Agnes grew in strength and beauty
And saved from annihilation
The white-horned birds

XV

The brain child
will not have blue eyes
Blue eyes are too green
and might fall in the sea
The sea of soap
which rolls new cigars
destined for guerilla lusts
hardly neglects the eyes
The eyes love copper
and copper is too green in the sea
So the eyes on the wing of an albatross
will leave the pale seas
for closed rooms
and will roll forever
on damned pianos

XVI

Grandie par la chaleur
la fillette solide
connaîtra les fleurs mâles
Bouche bouche et lèvres
l'amour des enfants vierges
aux scrupules indolents

XVII

Le toréador dit à la mariée
Bien sûr que je l'aime
Et la mariée se roula dans la sciure
une lanterne à la main
Sa main était sale
et la lanterne fragile
Qu'arriva-t-il qu'arriva-t-il
Un soldat accourut et lui fit un enfant
L'enfant était sale
comme les mains de sa mère
et aimait les lanternes fragiles
L'enfant était sale
et aimait les puits des châteaux
pour y jeter ses lanternes
qu'il appelait des soleils
quoiqu'elles fussent éteintes
Teintes teintes
répétait l'écho dans les couloirs
et l'enfant arrachait l'herbe
qu'l jetait dans les puits
C'est pour cela qu'il avait les mains sales

XVI

Larger from warmth
the solid little girl
will know the male flowers
Mouth mouth and lips
Love of virgin children
with indolent qualms

XVII

The toreador said to the bride
Of course I love you
And the bride rolled in sawdust
a lantern in her hand
her hand was dirty
and the lantern fragile
What happened what happened
A soldier ran over and knocked her up
The child was dirty
like his mother's hands
and liked fragile lanterns
The child was dirty
and liked the wells of castles
to throw in lanterns
that he called suns
although they were extinguished
Dyed dyed
repeated the echo in the corridors
and the child tore out the grass
and threw it in the well
That's why he had dirty hands

XVIII

A nous les petites femmes
dis-tu
Non
les petites femmes et les épines
sont pour les moujiks
Tu aimeras les serpents pour leur langue
et l'eau parce qu'elle coule entre les montagnes
Tu aimeras les serpents le dimanche seulement
et leur langue tous les jours
Les petites femmes n'aiment pas les moujiks
parce qu'ils sentent les allumettes
les petites femmes n'aiment que les feuilles
les feuilles sans coton
portant haut et fier le cadre de leur mère

XIX

Spectacle varié
La Source Saint-Ange
tarie par un caniche
Le caniche grossit grossit grossit grossit
et s'habilla de couleurs claires
On l'appelait Adam
Puisque Adam il y a
disons qu'il était chauve
et portait l'œil bleu
comme un monocle
Mais sur la source tarie
s'endormit un général plus grand que vieux
On l'appelait Bernadette
Il fumait fumait
et aimait les châteaux sans fenêtre
oh là là

XVIII

To us little girls
You say
No
little girls and thorns
are for the mujiks
You will love the serpents for their tongue
and water because it flows between the mountains
You will love the serpents Sunday only
and their tongue every day
The little girls do not like the mujiks
because they feel the matches
little girls only like leaves
leaves without cotton
carrying high and proudly the frame of their mother

XIX

Varied spectacle
Saint-Angel Springs
sapped by a poodle
the poodle grew grew grew grew
and dressed in light colors
He was named Adam
Since Adam it is
let's say that he was bald
and wore the blue eye
like a monocle
But on the dried up spring
slept a general bigger than old
They called him Bernadette
He smoked he smoked
and loved castles without windows
Ooh la la

PAUVRE BLÉ

Le roi disait à son peuple
Que chacun mette un pied en terre
et attende la floraison de l'autre
Et des pieds tendus sortirent des épis
beaux comme une horloge qui se trompe d'heure
Ils se balançaient aux soupirs du roi
Comme un navire antique
et leurs têtes s'entrechoquaient
avec un bruit de squelette descendant un escalier de pierre

Alors songeant que son peuple était mûr comme un général
le roi se leva de son trône
gifla la reine
et prenant la faulx son emblème
le hacha si menu
que le vent emporta pour toujours
un nuage de poussière blanche

POOR WHEAT

The king used to tell his people
Each one should put a foot in earth
and wait for the blossoming of the other one
And the stretched feet would emerge from the husks
beautiful like a clock that's wrong about the time
They swung on the sighs of the king
Like an antique ship
and their heads clattered
with the noise of a skeleton descending a stone staircase

So thinking that his people were mature like a general
the king rose from his throne
slapped the queen
and taking the sickle his emblem
chopped it so small
that the wind carried forever
a cloud of white powder

LES PUCES DU CHAMP

Laboure à tour de bras
Laboure les champs les rues les quais
et sèmes-y ce que tu voudras
des pavés de la fumée ou des bouteilles
mais laboure laboure comme un fou
et répands de l'engrais sur les pierres
pour y faire fleurir des drapeaux
mais qu'ils soient rouges
Les pluies et les vents te seront propices
si tu portes les aiguilles d'une montre à tes oreilles
et la récolte sera bonne comme la soupe de ta femme

Laboure ton champ et tous les autres
avec tes pieds avec ton nez
Défonce les haies comme un taureau
en chantant

Dans le Roussillon
il y avait un laboureur
qui sonnait de la bêche
il n'avait qu'une tête et deux bras
quatre pieds et deux yeux
une oreille et trois dents
mais c'était un laboureur
qui ne perdait pas son temps

THE FLEAS OF THE FIELD

Plough with all your might
Plough the fields streets wharves
and sow there what you would reap
from cobblestones smoke or bottles
but plough plough like a madman
and spread manure on the stones
to make flags flower there
but let them be red
The rains and the winds will be favorable to you
if you carry the hands of a watch to your ears
and the harvest will be good like your wife's soup

Plough your field and all the others
with your feet with your nose
Break down the hedges like a bull
singing

In the Roussillon
there was a plowman
who clanged the spade
he had only one head and two arms
four feet and two eyes
one ear and three teeth
but he was a plowman
who did not waste his time

QUE FONT LES OLIVES

Si tu me jettes des olives à la tête
une forêt naîtra sous mon crâne
afin qu'un jour tu t'y égares
comme une olive dans un dé à coudre

Dans la forêt il pleuvra des olives
qui connaissent le chemin de ma tête
ce chemin pavé de calcaires abattus
où la barbe d'un christ garde les ordures des passants
ce chemin qui tu connais mieux que la flamme celui de la maison
mieux que le poisson celui de l'hameçon
mieux que le chien celui du chat
mieux que la chaleur celui du thermomètre
et mieux que le coureur celui du pavé
Mais tu es sourd et lâche comme une branche morte
et ta voix charrie des coquilles vides
Et les olives le savent bien
Elles montent elles glissent le long des hanches
elles recouvrent ta poitrine tes épaules ta tête
Que les olives t'étouffent

WHAT THE OLIVES DO

If you throw olives at my head
a forest will be born under my skull
so that one day you will wander there
like an olive in a thimble

In the forest it will rain olives
which know the way to my head
that way paved with beaten cobblestones
where the beard of Christ guards the trash of passersby
that path that you know better than flame that of the house
better than the fish the that of the hook
better than the dog that of the cat
better than warmth that of the thermometer
and better than the runner that of the pavement
But you are deaf and cowardly like a dead branch
and your voice hauls empty shells
And the olives know it well
They climb they glide along the hips
they recover your chest your shoulders your head
May the olives smother you

TESTAMENT DE PARMENTIER

Pomme de terre qu'as-tu fait de ta mère

Ma mère était une putain
qui n'avait pas de robe de chambre

Pomme de terre qu'as-tu fait de ton père

Mon père était un ivrogne
qui m'écrasait sur son nez

Pomme de terre tu vas mourir
et ta peau drapera plus d'un fantôme
égaré dans de noirs escaliers
mais avant regarde-toi dans ton miroir
et dis-moi s'il va pleuvoir

TESTAMENT OF THE SHEPHERD'S PIE

Potato what have you done with your mother

My mother was a whore
who had no bathrobe

Potato what have you done with your father

My father was a drunk
who crushed me on his nose

Potato you are going to die
and your skin will drape more than one ghost
lost in gloomy staircases
but before that look at yourself in your mirror
and tell me if it's going to rain

SOMBRES VACHES

Paysan paysan lave tes pieds
Paysan paysan trais tes vaches
dans le ciboire du curé
Avec leurs cornes tu feras des christs
avec leurs sabots des bénitiers

Paysan paysan trais tes vaches avec ton pied
ton pied sale comme le christ
et ton lait s'en ira sur les montagnes
remplacer la neige

Paysan paysan tes vaches sont pourries
Leur sacré cœur n'est qu'une bouse
où picorent des moineaux

Paysan paysan tes vaches mangent le curé
Paysan paysan tes vaches sont dans l'église
et meuglent dans le confessionnal
Elles paissent les robes des bigotes
et montent dans la chaire

Celle qui est pleine met bras devant l'autel
et voici le nouveau fils de dieu qui vagit

Paysan paysan tes vaches sont chez elles

DARK COWS

Peasant peasant wash your feet
Peasant peasant milk your cows
into the wafer box of the curate
With their horns you will make christs
with their hooves fonts of holy water

Peasant peasant milk your cows with your foot
your foot dirty like christ
and your milk will go off onto the mountains
to replace snow

Peasant peasant your cows are rotten
Their sacred heart is nothing but a cowpie
where sparrows peck

Peasant peasant your cows are eating the priest
Peasant peasant your cows are in the church
and they are mooing in the confessional
They graze on the robes of the zealots
and climb into the pulpit

The one who's pregnant bears down before the altar
and here is the new son of god who weeps

Peasant peasant your cows are home

QUAND IL N'Y A PLUS DE FOIN DANS LE RÂTELIER

Si j'avais sur la tête tout le foin que j'ai coupé
que j'ai coupé en quatre
j'aurais une chevelure d'aube et de beurre frais
mais le foin coupé s'en va à la rivière
comme la plume au vent
Il la monte et la descend
sans savoir où il va
et les bateaux qui le pourchassent ne le rattraperont jamais
car le foin coupé a des ailes
des ailes qui le conduisent n'importe où
dans les palais et les prisons
dans la bouche des moines
dans l'oreille des sourds
dans le cou des condamnés à mort
sur les tombes illustres
et dans les théâtres subventionnés

WHEN THERE'S NO MORE HAY IN THE HAYRACK

If I had on my head all the hay that I've cut
that I've split
I'd have a head of hair of dawn and fresh butter
but the cut hay goes off to the river
like the feather in the wind
It rides it up and down
without knowing where it's going
and the boats that hunt it will never catch up
because the cut hay has wings
wings that lead it anywhere
into palaces and prisons
into the mouths of monks
into the ear of the deaf
into the neck of those condemned to die
on famous tombs
and into subsidized theatres

LA FORÊT SAOULE

Un arbre abattu ce sera pour toi
deux aussi
et la forêt de même
car une source coule de mon genou
emportant ma hache vers d'autres continents

Un arbre abattu ce sera pour toi
Qu'il pleuve vente ou neige
porte-le à ton cou
pour que ta vie soit chaude comme une braise

Que ma hache refleurisse dans sa forêt natale
ou qu'elle erre comme un vieux naufragé
au gré des morts subites
un arbre abattu ce sera pour toi

THE DRUNKEN FOREST

A felled tree this will be for you
two more
and the forest too
because a spring flows from my knee
bearing my axe away to other continents

A felled tree this will be for you
Come rain shine or snow
carry it around your neck
so that your life will be warm like embers

Whether my axe flowers again in its native forest
or whether it wanders like a shipwrecked old man
at the mercy of the sudden dead
a felled tree this will be for you

SANS TOMATES PAS D'ARTICHAUTS

Mes tomates sont plus mûres que tes sabots
et tes artichauts ressemblent à ma fille

Sur la place du marché
il y avait une tomate et un artichaut
et tous deux dansaient autour d'un navet
qui tournait sur sa racine

Dansez tomate dansez artichaut
le jour de vos noces sera clair comme le regard des carpes
Les sabots qui nous contemplent
en pleurent des larmes de poires blettes
et s'ils chantent ils font un bruit de cercueil
qui éclate et fait surgir un cadavre
Le cadavre bat des mains comme un caillou dans une vitre
et dit
Non tu n'auras pas ma tomate à ce prix-là

WITHOUT TOMATOES NO ARTICHOKES

My tomatoes are riper than your hooves
and your artichokes look like my daughter

At the marketplace
there was a tomato and an artichoke
and the two of them danced around a turnip
which spun on its root

Dance tomato dance artichoke
and the day of your marriage will be fair like the gaze of carp
The wooden shoes that contemplate us
cry about it with tears of overripe pears
and if they sing they make a noise of a coffin
that bursts and makes a corpse pop out
The corpse claps his hands like a pebble through a windowpane
and says
No you will not have my tomato at that price

A MOUTON TONDU MOUCHES HEUREUSES

Cinq ou six moutons perdus dans l'escaliers
L'un disait Je vais à la cave
un autre montait au grenier
un troisième sonnait à l'entresol
La porte ouvert il vit une tondeuse
qui fredonnait une romance de fils télégraphiques
La tondeuse était grande et belle comme une jeune haie
Ses yeux étaient si lumineux
que le mouton songea Mais c'est ma sœur
la tabatière du patron
Et sa voix se fit persuasive
comme la sirène d'un navire en perdition
la marée montante
ou la lettre revenue avec la mention DÉCÉDÉ
Elle disait cette voix Les moutons sont de braves gens
Sans tambour ni trompette ils viennent et s'en vont
Ils partent avec du poil et reviennent sans chemise
Vivent les moutons bien tondus

TO SHEARED SHEEP HAPPY FLIES

Five or six sheep lost in the staircases
One of them said I'm going to the cellar
another climbed to the attic
a third rang at the main floor
The door open he saw a pair of shears
which hummed a romance of telegraphic wires
The shears were big and beautiful like a young hedge
Its eyes were so luminous
that the sheep thought But that's my sister
the snuff box of the boss
And its voice was so persuasive
like the siren of a ship in distress
the waves rising
or the letter returned with the note DECEASED
It was speaking this voice The sheep are brave people
Without drum or trumpet they come and they go
They leave with hair and come back shirtless
Long live the well-sheared sheep

CHANSON DE LA SÉCHERESSE

Va-t-il pleuvoir ciel de pendu
s'il pleut je mangerai du cresson
s'il ne pleut pas de la langouste

Va-t-il pleuvoir ciel du voyou
s'il pleut tu auras des frites
s'il ne pleut pas la prison

Va-t-il pleuvoir ciel d'andouille
s'il pleut tu auras un oignon
s'il ne pleut pas du vinaigre

Va-t-il pleuvoir ciel de gendarme
s'il pleut tu auras un âne
s'il ne pleut pas un putois

Va-t-il pleuvoir ciel de cocu
s'il pleut j'aurai ta femme
s'il ne pleut pas tes filles

Va-t-il pleuvoir ciel de curé
s'il pleut tu seras occis
s'il ne pleut pas tu seras brûlé

Va-t-il pleuvoir ciel d'étable
s'il pleut tu auras des pierres
s'il ne pleut pas des mouches

Va-t-il pleuvoir ciel de sorcière
s'il pleut tu auras un peigne
s'il ne pleut pas une pelle

SONG OF THE DROUGHT

Is it going to rain sky of the hanged man
if it rains I'll eat watercress
if it doesn't rain crayfish

Is it going to rain sky of the punk
if it rains you'll have fries
if it doesn't rain prison

Is it going to rain sky of sausage
if it rains you'll have an onion
if it doesn't rain some vinegar

Is it going to rain sky of policeman
if it rains you'll have an ass
if it doesn't rain a skunk

Is it going to rain sky of cuckold
if it rains I will have your wife
if it doesn't rain your daughters

Is it going to rain sky of the priest
if so you'll be slain
if not you'll be burned

Is it going to rain sky of barn
if it rains you'll have stones
if it doesn't rain you'll have flies

Is it going to rain sky of the sorceror
if it rains you'll have a comb
if not a shovel

Va-t-il pleuvoir ciel d'égoût
s'il pleut tu auras un drapeau
s'il ne pleut pas un crucifix

Va-t-il pleuvoir ciel de cendre

Is it going to rain sky of sewer
if it rains you'll have a flag
if it doesn't rain a crucifix

Is it going to rain sky of ash

Le passager du transatlantique

The Transatlantic Passenger

EN AVANT

En avant disait l'arc-en-ciel matinal
En avant pour les soupiraux de notre jeunesse
Nous avons éclaté
et tout ce qui était bleu est resté bleu

En souvenir des petits oignons
que tu mettais dans les chrysanthèmes
dis bonjour à la dame

Avant casse ta tête
ou celle de ton voisin le plus proche
en sorte que tous les deux
nous prendrons l'Orient-Express aux prochaines vacances

FORWARD

Full speed ahead said the morning rainbow
Ahead to the vents of our youth
We have exploded
and everything that was blue has stayed blue

In memory of little onions
that you put in the chrysanthemums
say hello to the lady

First smash your face
or your nearest neighbor's
so that that both of us
will take the Orient Express on our next vacation

PETIT HUBLOT DE MON CŒUR

Canada canada
mon petit canada
C'est la pomme la pomme qu'il nous faut
la pomme du Canada
la reine du Canada
reinette du Canada
C'est la reine qu'il nous faut
la reine dans son panier
dans son panier percé
Son Canada sous son bras
la reine s'en alla
et la reinette du Canada
son chapeau percé
son panier sous son bras
ses pieds dans ses sabots
elle chantait
Lorsque le pélican pélican lassé d'un long long voyage long
    voyage long voyage
et partit du pied gauche

LITTLE WINDOW OF MY HEART

Canada canada
my little canada
It's the apple the apple we need
the apple of Canada
the queen of Canada
golden apple of Canada
It's the queen we need
the queen in her basket
in her pierced basket
Her Canada under her arm
the queen went away
and the golden apple of Canada
her hat pierced
her basket under her arm
her feet in her clogs
was singing
While the pelican pelican weary from a long long voyage long
    voyage long voyage
and left with the left foot

EN ARRIÈRE

Sans hésitation ni murmure
le prince n'hésite pas
il craint les chutes sur la glace
La princesse qui a la migraine
hésite lorsqu'elle est majestueuse
C'est pourquoi le prince
voulait qu'on fasse machine arrière

FROM BEHIND

Without hesitation or murmur
the prince does not hesitate
he fears falls on the ice
The princess who has a migraine
hesitates when she is majestic
That's why the prince
wanted to back up

PASSERELLE DU COMMANDANT

Il faut être chaste pour être bon
Il faut être vieux pour savoir faire
Il faut être riche pour tous les temps
Il faut être grand pour regarder
Il faut être juste pour installer
Il faut être bien pour supporter
Il faut être rond pour mesurer
Il faut être tendre pour concourir
Il faut être seul pour opérer
Il faut être deux pour être trois

THE COMMANDER'S GANGWAY

You must be chaste to be good
You must be old to know how
You must be rich for all times
You must be tall to look
You must be fair to settle in
You must be well to withstand
You must be round to measure
You must be tender to compete
You must be alone to operate
You must be two to be three

PONT AUX CYGNES

Quel âge Quelle heure Quel temps
Quel âge Merci c'est un secret
Quelle heure Elles sont toutes bonnes
meilleures que les pralines du docteur Docteur
Quel temps celui des oreilles chaudes
des mains chaudes
du cœur chaud
ainsi que du reste

BRIDGE OF SWANS

How old What time What weather
How old Thanks it's a secret
What time Hours are all fair
better than the pralines of doctor Doctor
What weather that of warm ears
warm hands
warm heart
and so on etc

DRAPEAU DES MAINS SALES

A Georges Ribemont-Dessaignes.

Il était un petit drapeau
il avait deux deux œufs sur l'oreille oreille oreille
chantait une dame
qui
     craignait des courants d'air
     buvait ce qu'elle buvait
     mangeait ce qu'elle pouvait
     disait ce qu'elle savait
et bien d'autres choses qui n'intéressent personne
hormis deux vieux messieurs
agents de la préfecture de police

FLAG OF DIRTY HANDS

To Georges Ribemont-Dessaignes

It was a little flag
it had two two eggs on the ear ear ear
was singing a lady
who
    feared drafts of air
    drank what she drank
    ate what she could
    said what she knew
and many other things that interested no one
besides two old men
agents of the prefect of police

CHAUFFERIE MÉLANCOLIQUE

A Théodore Fraenkel.

Je rêve à toutes les étoiles
et elles en font autant
Il n'y a pas de temps à perdre
tout cela va éclater
Nous sommes perdus
nous somme perclus
Soupirer ou regarder
pas du tout je ne rêve plus et je m'en vais
Nous ne sommes pas perdus

MELANCHOLY BOILER ROOM

To Théodore Fraenkel

I dream of all the stars
and they do the same
There's no time to lose
everything's going to blow
We're lost
we're crippled
To sigh or look
not at all I dream no more and I'm going away
We're not lost

TIMONERIE DES VIEUX GÉNIES

A Arp.

Je n'ai qu'un œil et deux cerveaux
et vous comment va votre oreille
Ils sont partis mais ils s'arrêteront
Il n'y a pas de raison pour qu'ils continuent
il n'y a pas de routes
les routes ne sont pas sûres
les routes ne sont pas larges
Prenez garde à votre droite
dit le code pénal
Avec la mesure d'une peine progressive
nous atteindrons quelque sommet un jour ou l'autre
ce sont des choses qui se vérifient
Addition soustraction multiplication et division

QUARTERMASTER OF OLD GENIUSES

To Arp

I only have one eye and two brains
and you how's your ear
They've left but they'll stop
There's no reason for them to go on
there are no roads
the roads are uncertain
the roads are not wide
Look out on your right
says the penal code
With the measure of a growing sorrow
we will reach some summit one day or other
these are things that can be proved
Addition subtraction multiplication and division

BÂBORD POUR TOUS

Bâbord détachez mon cerveau bleu
Bâbord éloignez mon voisin de gauche
Bâbord donnez-moi de l'eau potable
Bâbord prenez garde aux montagnes
Bâbord songez à l'arsenic
Bâbord changez l'encre qui est jaune
Bâbord protégez-moi des courants d'air
Bâbord souvenez-vous de l'année dernière
Bâbord souvenez-vous de la chaleur
Bâbord souvenez-vous des promeneurs de cactus
car nous passons
nous passons et les hirondelles passent avec nous
mais nous crachons en l'air
et les hirondelles crachent sur nous

PORT SIDE FOR ALL

Port unleash my blue brain
Port push back my neighbor on the left
Port give me drinkable water
Port watch out for the mountains
Port dream of arsenic
Port change the ink it's yellow
Port protect me from currents of air
Port remember last year
Port remember heat
Port remember the walkers on cactus
because we move past
we move past and the swallows go with us
but we spit in the air
and the swallows spit on us

TRIBORD ASIATIQUE

Les œufs sont cassés
et le réveille-matin ne sonne plus
Veux-tu me dire pourquoi
tu veux rester tranquille
Ah ça ne me regarde pas et toi non plus

Le bateau penche sur tribord
Les œufs ne sont pas cassés
Le réveille-matin sonne huit heures dix
A bon entendeur salut

ASIATIC STARBOARD

The eggs are broken
and the alarm clock no longer rings
Do you want to tell me why
you want to stay quiet
Ah that doesn't concern me or you

The boat lists toward starboard
The eggs are not broken
The alarm clock sounds eight ten
A word to the wise

HOMME DE QUART
HOMME DE DEMI

A Jacques Rigaut.

Mystère de l'homme ou réciproquement

Pour expliquer que faut-il
Deux hommes et trois poissons
C'est un mystère

Pour diminuer que faut-il
Être sûr de son âge
C'est un mystère

Pour augmenter que faut-il
Marcher ou descendre ou monter
C'est un mystère

Terre

QUARTER MAN
HALF MAN

To Jacques Rigaut

Mystery of man or reciprocally

To explain what do we need
Two men and three fish
It's a mystery

To shrink what do we need
To be sure of one's age
It's a mystery

To grow what do we need
To walk or go down or climb
It's a mystery

Earth

PASSAGERS DE PREMIÈRE CLASSE ET LEUR TEINT FRAIS

Samuel Altiber naquit en 1622
le 17 du mois de mars je crois
le 18 mars il disait
Samuel Altiber
et son père le croirez-vous
lui fit fumer une pipe de tabac des Indes

FIRST CLASS PASSENGERS AND THEIR FRESH COMPLEXION

Samuel Altiber was born in 1622
the 17th of the month of March I believe
the 18th of March he said
Samuel Altiber
and his father will you believe it
made him smoke a pipe of tobacco from the Indies

PASSAGERS DE SECONDE CLASSE ET LEURS CHEVEUX

J'y cours
Où courez-vous
Nulle part
Moi aussi
Alors

SECOND CLASS PASSENGERS AND THEIR HAIR

I'm running there
Where are you running
Nowhere
Me too
So

ÉMIGRANT DES MILLE MILLES

A Jacques Vaché.

Boulevard Sébastopol ou Wilhelmstrasse
nos sœurs sont deux putains

L'annonce disait ou laissait dire
qu'à partir de vingt-sept ans on entendait mieux
J n'ai pas le même âge que toi
et mon frère non plus

On voit que vous n'êtes pas de la partie
Qu'est-ce qu'un cancer
Qu'est-ce que le génie
C'est la même chose
et le caoutchouc aussi
mais dites-moi ce qu'est le caoutchouc

EMIGRANT OF THE THOUSAND NAUTICAL MILES

To Jacques Vaché

Boulevard Sébastopol or Wilhelmstrasse
our sisters are two whores

The declaration was saying or let it be implied
that from 27 years old one could hear better
I am not the same age as you
neither is my brother

We see that you are not with us
What's a cancer
What's genius
It's the same thing
and rubber too
but tell me what's rubber

ALARME MAL CALCULÉE

Nous sommes loin ou alors
Il y a de l'eau qu'on ne boit pas
c'est de l'eau potable
Il y a des gens qu'on ne voit pas
ce sont les morts
on ne les entend pas non plus
Pourquoi prétendez-vous le contraire
Pourquoi avez-vous crié si fort
vous voyez bien que nous allons mourir
moi je n'y tiens pas

ALARM BADLY PLANNED

We're a long way or what
There's water we can't drink
it's drinkable water
There are folks we don't see
these are the dead
we don't hear them any more
Why do you pretend the contrary
Why did you shout so loudly
you see clearly that we're going to die
me I don't want to

BAR POUR BAR
FUMOIR POUR FUMOIR

Mesure impartialement celui qui mesure C'est le cri du cœur approuva le commis-voyageur qui avait rangé ses sentiments dans un écrin de cuir fauve fermé par une serrure dont il ignorait le secret Ce secret était contenu dans un livre érotique du XIe siècle Il n'était autre que le douzième mot de la quatrième ligne de la cent cinquante-quatrième page

Passons à un autre exercice et avouons-nous qu'ils ne sont pas variés Le rocking-chair ou la logique ne sort jamais d'un certain espace car il s'endort

Brise une table et dis que c'est l'œuvre de ton ami Brisons là vous aurez mes témoins C'est toujours la même chose l'esprit française l'esprit des reliques l'esprit saint

En usez-vous Jamais de la vie l'abus avant tout liqueurs fortes pour estomacs de jeunesse musique des pompiers et de la garde républicaine qui fait bâiller les chaussures

Il est temps vous rendez-vous compte qu'il est temps Alors pourquoi regardez-vous votre café qui fait des petits bonds saccadés Nouveau sport pensez-vous vous avez tort au quatorzième siècle etc

Couper quatre cheveux en un Réfléchissez-y bien réfléchissez-y bien et sans logique de crainte d'accidents Alors vous allez voir que tout sera changé les objets animés auront des mouvements convulsifs votre fourchette dansera devant vos yeux le fox-trot du jour Ce sera le jour du fox-trot le jour des abbés le jour de l'emprunt Mais vous quand aurez-vous votre jour C'est simple mourez d'abord

348

BAR FOR BAR
SMOKING ROOM FOR SMOKING ROOM

Measure impartially whoever measures It's the heart's cry approved the commercial traveler who had put away his feelings in a tan leather case closed by a lock whose secret he didn't know This secret was contained in an erotic book of the 11th century It was none other than the twelfth word of the fourth line of the one hundred and fifty-fourth page

Let's move on to another exercise and confess that they do not vary The rocking chair or logic never leave a certain space because it falls asleep

Break a table and say that's the work of your friend Let's break there you will have my witnesses It's always the same thing French spirit spirit of relics holy spirit

Are you using it up Never in my life abuse above all strong liqueurs for stomachs of youth music of the firemen and of the republican guard which makes shoes yawn

It's time do you realize that it's time So why are you looking at your coffee which makes little jerky leaps New sport are you thinking You're wrong in the fourteenth century etc

Cut four hairs in one Think about it hard think about it hard and without logic of fear of accidents So you're going to see that all will be changed lively objects will have convulsive movements your fork will dance before your eyes the foxtrot of the day That will be the day of the foxtrot the day of the abbeys the day of the loan But you when will you have your day It's simple die first

Au feu Au feu Ne craignez rien ce n'est pas dangereux tout brûle et tout s'éteint l'éternité n'est pas de ce côté Tournez la tête tournez bien la tête voyez-vous Non Eh bien vous avez tort et couchez-vous

Vous sentez vos cheveux pousser et vois concluez que nous approchons de l'équinoxe du printemps Ce serait peut-être vrai ailleurs mais ici où les clowns sont des banquiers et des évêques qui ont la peau dure et les souvenirs amers

Au surplus je ne vois pas pourquoi nous causons de cela

Fire Fire Have no fear it is not dangerous everything burns and everything dies out eternity is not on earth Turn your head really turn your head do you see No Oh well you're wrong and lie down

You feel your hair grow and you conclude that we're approaching the spring equinox That would be perhaps true somewhere elsewhere but here where clowns are bankers and bishops who have tough skin and bitter memories

Moreover I do not see why we're talking about that

BENJAMIN PÉRET (1899–1959)

Born July 4, 1899, in Rezé, near Nantes. His mother was from Southern Brittany, on the border of La Vendée; his father, a civil servant, came from the South of France. His poems include images of oceans and ships, forests, wildflowers and grasses.

His parents divorced when he was two years old, and he was raised by his mother.

July 31, 1913: Restless and unsuccessful in school, he quit L'Ecole Livet, did not attend the *lycée* (high school). These days he might be tested for Attention Deficit Disorder; in 1913 he was probably just smacked around and told he was no good.

1914–1918: Arrested for painting a town statue, he was given a choice of jail or the army. According to most accounts, his mother pushed him to join the army. He was deployed to the Balkans, contracted severe dysentery in Salonica and was later repatriated in Lorraine. Along the way, he found *Sic* magazine on a railway bench and discovered Apollinaire's poetry. November 1918, his first poem, "Crépuscule," was published in a youth literary magazine, *Tramontane.*

1920: Went to Paris to "launch a literary career." Tristan Tzara also arrived in Paris at this time. Mid-January, Péret showed up at André Breton's apartment. He met with Breton, Eluard, Aragon, and Soupault at the "First Friday of *Littérature*," where they were planning Dadaist events. Péret had been reading Rimbaud.

1921: May 13, as part of Dadaist demonstrations, Péret dressed as the Unknown Soldier at the mock trial of Barrès. April 14, the Dadaists visited Saint-Julien-le-Pauvre in a mock publicity event. Péret published *Le passager du transatlantique,* illustrated by Hans Arp (Collections Dada). Péret used the technique of automatic writing for this volume.

1922: French poets and artists broke with Dadaism. "Dadaism is not a beginning but an end" (Péret). The time of "sleeping fits" took hold; trances and automatic writing sessions at Breton's apartment became routine. Crevel, Desnos, and Péret were stars; a woman whom Péret was dating also fell into a trance.

1923: *Au 125 du boulevard Saint-Germain,* illustrated by Max Ernst, included three drawings by Péret (*Littérature*).

1924: Founding of *La Revolution surréaliste,* journal of the Surrealist movement, which supplanted Dada. Directors: Pierre Naville and Benjamin Péret. *Immortelle maladie,* frontispiece by Man Ray (*Littérature*).

1925: Exhibit by Miró in Paris, prefaced by Péret. The Surrealists were reading *Lenin,* by Leon Trotsky. They networked with the communists of *Clarté* magazine. Péret's "A travers mes yeux" appeared in the new series of *Littérature* 5; published *Il était une boulangère* (Sagittaire) and *152 proverbes mis au goût du jour* with the collaboration of Paul Eluard (Éd. Surréal.)

1926: Worked with *Humanité* magazine, signed anti-clerical and anti-military articles.

1927: *Dormir, dormir, dans les pierres,* illustrated by Tanguy (Éd. Surréal), January 31. In May, *Au grand jour* appeared, a pamphlet of Surrealist writings supporting the Communist Party.

1928: *Le grand jeu* (Gallimard) appeared originally with a frontispiece photograph of the author by Man Ray. The original volume was dedicated to André Breton.
    April 12, married Brazilian singer Elsie Houston in Paris.
    Adherence to Trotsky's leftist Opposition.

1929: *Et les seins mouraient* (Cahiers du Sud), frontispiece by Miró. Published *1929* with Aragon and photos by Man Ray, this volume of sexually explicit poems and photographs was banned in France.

Mid-February 1929, departed with Elsie for Sao Paolo. Series of conferences and articles on Surrealism.

1929–1931: Péret lived in Brazil. His political activity resulted in his imprisonment. November 30–January 31, he translated into Portuguese Trostky's *Litteratéur et Révolution*.

August 31, 1931, his son Geyser Péret was born in Rio.

December 10, 1931, he was expelled from Brazil for communist activism.

1932: Returned to France, worked as a copy editor. Participated in Surrealist activity.

Refused to declare Surrealism "counter-revolutionary" and was denied membership in the Ligue, the Communist League.

1933: Separated from Elsie Houston, who returned to Brazil with Geyser.

1934: *De derrière les fagots* (Éd. Surréal.), illustrated by Max Ernst.

1935–36: Péret and Breton organized an international exposition of Surrealism in the Canary Islands.

June 2, rejoined the International Worker's party (Trotskyite).

August 1935, Péret reached Spain at the beginning of the civil war and agitated against Franco in the ranks of the P.O.U.M. (anti-Stalinist communist party), and then saw combat as part of Durruti's anarchist column.

Met Remedios Varo in Barcelona, a painter who became his companion and whom he will later marry.

January 1936, published *Je ne mange pas ce pain-là* (Éd. Surréal.) and *Je sublime* (Éd. Surréal).

1937: April, 1937, returned to Spain. Published *Trois cerises et une sardine* (G.L.M.)

1938: *Au paradis des fantômes.* (Éd. Un Divertissement)

1940: Drafted in February, sent to Paris and then to Nantes. Imprisoned in Rennes for political activity, bribed his way out and was released on June 21st in the wake of the arrival of German troops. Went to Paris.

March, took refuge in Marseilles, participated in Surrealist activities with Breton at Villa Air Bel.

1941: October, he and Remedios Varo left for Mexico, stopped in Casablanca, arrived in Vera-Cruz in mid-December.

1942: Gatherings with artists and writers included Leonora Carrington and Octavio Paz.

Published *Les malheurs d'un dollar* (Main à Plume).

March 1943: Elsie Houston committed suicide in New York.

Published *La parôle est à Péret* (Éd. Surréal.) Wrote about the ways that poetry and the imagination helped him to survive prison. He asserted that poetry's goal is the liberation of human beings.

February 1945: *Le déshonneur des poètes* (written in Mexico, published in Paris, Alain Gheerbrant); *Dernier malheur, dernier chance* (L'Age d'or).

1946: May 10, Married Remedios Varo in Cholulo, Mexico, state of Puebla.

Published *Main forte*, illustrated by Victor Brauner (Fontaine).

1947: *Feu central*, illustrated by Tanguy (K).

1948: Separated from Remedios Varo, Péret returned to Paris alone. Broke with the Fourth Internationale and rejoined the Union of International Workers.

1949: *La brebis galante*, illustrated by Max Ernst (Éd. Premières).

1952: *Air Mexicain*, illustrated by Tamayo (Arcanes).

1953: *Mort aux vaches et au champ d'honneur* (Arcanes).

1954: *Les rouilles encageés* (under the pseudon. of Satyremont, ed. E. Losfeld).

1955: *Le livre de Chilám Bilám de Chumayel* (Denoël), Péret's translation of the Mayan epic. Péret left for Brazil and lived with tribal people in the Amazon.

1956: *Anthologie de l'amour sublime* (Albin Michel), preceded by *Noyau de la comète*.

1957: *Le gigot, sa vie, son oeuvre* (Éd. Le Terrain Vague).

1958: *Histoire naturelle* (anonymous, Ussel) *La poesie surrealista francese* (Milan, Schwarz).

1959: Operated on twice for arterial blockages, Péret died in Boucicaut Hospital of heart failure, September 18, 1959. His tomb at Batignolles cemetery bears the inscription: Benjamin Péret (1899–1959) JE NE MANGE PAS DE CE PAIN-LA.

1960: Appearance of *L'Anthologie des mythes, legends et contes populaires d'Amerique* (Albin Michel), written in 1955.

1963: Publication of *Dames et généraux* (Milan: Schwarz; Paris, Berggeron).

1965: Publication of *Pour un second manifest communiste,* with Munis (Éd. Le Terrain Vague).

1968: Publication of *Les Mains dans les poches* (Montpellier: Leo Editeur), and of *Syndicats contre la révolution,* with G. Munis (Éd. Le Terrain Vague).

1969: *Oeuvres complètes,* I, *Poèsie,* Preface by André Breton from his *Anthologie de l'humour noir* (Losfeld).

1971: Tome II, *Poèsie* (Losfeld).

1979: Tome III, *Contes,* Preface by Octavio Paz (Losfeld).

1987: Tome IV, *Contes—Oeuvres en collaboration* (Losfeld).

1989: Tome V, *Textes politiques* (José Corti).

1992: Tome VI, *Les Ameriques…et autres lieux—le Cinématographie—Les Arts plastiques* (José Corti).

1995: Tome VII, *Le déshonneur des poètes*; *Textes divers—Correspondance—Bibliographie* (José Corti).

MARILYN KALLET is the author of fifteen books, including *Packing Light: New and Selected Poems* and has translated Paul Eluard's *Last Love Poems,* both from Black Widow Press. She is director of the creative writing program at the University of Tennessee, where she holds a Lindsay Young Professorship. She also teaches poetry workshops for the Virginia Center for the Creative Arts in Auvillar, France.

In 2005, Kallet was inducted into the East Tennessee Literary Hall of Fame in poetry, and named Woman of Achievement in the Arts by the YWCA in 2000. She has performed her poetry in theaters and on campuses across the United States, as well as in Warsaw and Krakow, as a guest of the US Embassy's "America Presents" program.

TITLES FROM BLACK WIDOW PRESS

TRANSLATION SERIES

Approximate Man and Other Writings
by Tristan Tzara. Translated and edited by
Mary Ann Caws.

Art Poétique by Guillevic.
Translated by Maureen Smith.

The Big Game by Benjamin Péret.
Translated with an introduction by Marilyn Kallet.

Capital of Pain by Paul Eluard.
Translated by Mary Ann Caws, Patricia Terry,
and Nancy Kline.

Chanson Dada: Selected Poems by Tristan Tzara.
Translated with an introduction and essay by
Lee Harwood.

*Essential Poems and Writings of Joyce Mansour:
A Bilingual Anthology*
Translated with an introduction by Serge
Gavronsky.

Essential Poems and Prose of Jules Laforgue
Translated and edited by Patricia Terry.

*Essential Poems and Writings of Robert Desnos:
A Bilingual Anthology*
Edited with an introduction and essay by
Mary Ann Caws.

EyeSeas (Les Ziaux) by Raymond Queneau.
Translated with an introduction by Daniela
Hurezanu and Stephen Kessler.

Furor and Mystery & Other Writings by René Char.
Edited and translated by Mary Ann Caws and
Nancy Kline.

The Inventor of Love & Other Writings
by Gherasim Luca. Translated by Julian and Laura
Semilian. Introduction by Andrei Codrescu. Essay
by Petre Răileanu.

La Fontaine's Bawdy
by Jean de la Fontaine. Translated with an
introduction by Norman R. Shapiro.

Last Love Poems of Paul Eluard
Translated with an introduction by Marilyn Kallet.

Love, Poetry (L'amour la poésie)
by Paul Eluard. Translated with an essay by
Stuart Kendall.

Poems of André Breton: A Bilingual Anthology
Translated with essays by Jean-Pierre Cauvin
and Mary Ann Caws.

Poems of A.O. Barnabooth
by Valéry Larbaud.
Translated by Ron Padgett and Bill Zavatsky.

Preversities: A Jacques Prévert Sampler
Translated and edited by Norman R. Shapiro.

The Sea and Other Poems by Guillevic. Translated
by Patricia Terry. Introduction by Monique
Chefdor.

To Speak, to Tell You?
Poems by Sabine Sicaud. Translated by Norman
R. Shapiro. Introduction and notes by Odile
Ayral-Clause.

forthcoming translations

Essential Poems and Writings of Pierre Reverdy
Translated by Mary Ann Caws. Translated by
Mary Ann Caws, Patricia Terry, Ron Padgett,
and John Ashberry.

A Life of Poems, Poems of a Life
by Anna de Noailles. Translated by Norman R.
Shapiro. Introduction by Catherine Perry.